I HOPE I JOIN THE BAND

I HOPE I JOIN THE BAND

*Narrative, Affiliation, and
Antiracist Rhetoric*

FRANKIE CONDON

UTAH STATE UNIVERSITY PRESS
Logan
2012

Utah State University Press
Logan, Utah 84322-7800
© 2012 Utah State University Press
All rights reserved

Manufactured in the United States of America
Cover design by Barbara Yale-Read

ISBN: 978-0-87421-876-3 paper
ISBN: 978-0-87421-877-0 ebook

Library of Congress Cataloging-in-Publication Data

Condon, Frankie.
  I hope I join the band : narrative, affiliation, and antiracist rhetoric / Frankie Condon.
    p. cm.
  Includes bibliographical references and index.
  ISBN 978-0-87421-876-3 (pbk.) – ISBN 978-0-87421-877-0 (e-book)
1. Anti-racism. 2. Rhetoric–Social aspects. 3. Racism. 4. Racism in literature. 5. Racism-
-Study and teaching. I. Title.
  HT1521.C565 2012
  305.8–dc23
                          2011048146

FOR RICK

CONTENTS

ACKNOWLEDGMENTS

It is customary at such moments in a book to write, "This work could not have been completed without . . ." and so on. And yet, how else can one begin. No one writes alone, despite the stories we tell one another about how lonely writing is, about how isolated we may feel or may tell ourselves we are as we write. At no time is this more true than when writing of antiracism, *where* we are always accompanied by others, haunted by those who have come before us, and called by those who will come after. Finally, the work cannot be done well unless we recognize and honor, acknowledge, and attend to those who are already with us in the struggle.

This work could not have been completed without the love, friendship, support, and intellectual engagement of a great many people. I have been the beneficiary of a great activist education. Nadya Lawson and Naomi Jaffe first invited me to join an antiracist organization and to participate in antiracist leadership training through the Dismantling Racism Project in Albany, New York. My friend, Jennifer Mitchell, also a member of the DRP, has for too many years to count now been my sounding board, a gentle critic, a cajoler when I grow tired, and an inspiration every day. The leaders, laborers, and workshop facilitators of Training for Change in Philadelphia offered me still more antiracist education and leadership preparation. Michael Dickel, then at Macalester College, invited me to attend a leadership training led by facilitators from the People's Institute for Survival and Beyond that was transformative for me, both personally and as an activist and writer. My former St. Cloud State University colleague, Debra Leigh, invited me to join a leadership team of antiracist community activists and educators. As a part of that group, with the guidance of Carmen Valenzuela and James Addington, I learned in much greater detail not only about institutional and systemic racism, but about organizing for change, thinking and acting strategically toward change, and about listening, speaking, and acting toward transformational as well as transactional change at individual, group, and institutional levels. And it is through the support of Carmen and James that I first began to think much more deeply and carefully about transracial friendship, alliance, solidarity, and activism.

I have been blessed by colleagues at colleges and universities across the country, who have taught me and supported my work on this book. Thanks go to my former coauthors, Elizabeth Boquet, Meg Carroll, Anne Ellen Geller, and Michele Eodice, who are always with me now whenever I am writing. Michele read, responded, and mentored me all the way through the writing of this book and, without her support, I never would have finished the work. I need also to thank Kami Day, Beth Godbee, Moira Ozias, Rasha Diab, Tanya Cochran, Jay Sloan, Nicole Munday, Andrew Rihn, Clint Gardner, Therese Thonus, and Zanice Bond de Perez. Harry Denny read and responded kindly and compellingly to early chapter drafts. Vershawn Young has been companion and interlocutor, guide and fellow traveler, throughout the writing of the book, and his contributions to the work, which run throughout, have made it far better than I ever could have done alone. I owe thanks to the anonymous reviewers of the manuscript, who gave such generous, fair, and challenging feedback. Michael Spooner, Director of Utah State University Press, offered trust in the value of the project and incisive questions at critical moments in the writing of it. Michael's support has been invaluable and his friendship is most dear to me. Another friend, Amy Scherer, has been my outside-academia support, always showing interest and, as a fellow skating mom, never, ever doing any of the things I diss the parents of rink rats for in the book.

My colleagues on and off the Community Anti-Racism Education Initiative at St. Cloud State University and in the

City of St. Cloud helped me tremendously through many challenging years of study and of activism. Catherine Fox, Margaret Villanueva, Mike Tripp, Karen Flynn, Eddah Mutua-Kombo, Geoffrey Tabakin, Tamrat Tademe, and Tracy Ore, among many others, listened, engaged, critiqued, laughed, and cried with me through much of the emergent thinking I did in preparation for writing this book. Rex Veeder has been my constant friend, my confidante, and the poet-artist who has offered his vision and understanding through all the years of writing *I Hope I Join the Band*.

I could not have written this book without the opportunities for teaching, research, and writing I have been afforded at the University of Nebraska-Lincoln, by the English department, and by my colleagues. My writing group, Amelia Montes, Joy Castro, and Barbara DiBernardi, listened and gave feedback and support during the early drafting of the manuscript. Chris Gallagher, Debbie Minter, Shari Stenberg, Amy Goodburn, June Griffin, and Robert Brooke have all asked hard questions and leaned in to let me process as I searched for answers. My new colleagues, Stacey Waite and Brie Owens, offered me not only friendship (which is spectacular), but also sounding-board and copyediting assistance in the final revising stages.

I have been blessed over the years to work with undergraduate and graduate students who have taught me far more than I could ever have taught them. From my earliest days directing the writing center at Siena College, working with Jill Casey, Elizabeth Byrne, and Christine Hutchinson and so many more, to St. Cloud State University and working with Brandon Bufe, Katie Peppers, Menan Jengu, and Poorni Gawarammana, I have been coached with good humor and great intelligence by my students. Over the years since I arrived at the University of Nebraska-Lincoln, I have been honored to work with some terrific graduate students, all of whom have gently and kindly schooled me even as they've studied with me the range of problems and questions I have tried to take up in this book. I need especially to thank Mike Kelly, who talked and listened in the early days with both curiosity and patience. In a variety of ways Sandy Tarabochia, Alison Friedow, Travis Adams, Charise Alexander, Mevi Hova, D.J. Kim, Hye-Ran Jung, and Amy Schiffbauer supported and challenged me such that the book is better for their presence in the process of composing it. Bobbi Olson, Kelly Meyer, Bernice Olivas, and Jessica Rivera gave unflagging support, reading chapters and consulting with me over them, assisting me with source material, posing terrifically wicked questions, and staying with me during the searching time that followed.

I could not have written as I have, or written anything at all, without the love and support of my family. My sister, Mia, gave generously of her time to help with child- and eldercare in order that I might write. My mom told her stories and listened to my versions, helping me to flesh them out and thresh them through. My mom and my sister leaned in and listened with care and compassion, checking my stories for accuracy. But they also let go of stories we share, allowing me to tell them in my own way even when they interpreted events differently than I. My children, Dan, Lucy, and Grace, have all made tremendous sacrifices in order that this book might be written. In the questions they ask, the observations they make, and the stories they tell, I have found sustenance, inspiration, and still more education.

To the extent that I have been able to be bold, to do what I want and need to do, to both risk and yield myself to the work of writing and of activism, I have been able because of the boundless generosity and the abiding love of my husband, Mike. In June of 1995, Mike and I promised each other that we would share our lives openly with one another, speak the truth to one another in love, and honor and encourage one another's fulfillment as individuals through all the changes in our lives. Mike has kept these promises steadfastly, with extraordinary intelligence and kindness. There is a love that is grace: a love that, as Manning Marable would say, "redefines the limits of possibility." This is the love Mike gives. The writing of this book is but a small portion of what that love makes possible. For this, and for it all, I am grateful to infinity and beyond and back again.

Finally, I need to thank my brother, Rick. Although long miles and years, trouble and heartache, separate us, you are always my best friend.

Frankie Condon
March 2012

1

INTRODUCTION

One autumn day, I was driving my daughter Grace to a figure-skating lesson in Omaha. The journey would consume most of an hour and I was using the time to think about the keynote address I was scheduled to deliver at the National Conference on Peer Tutoring in Writing. The conference was less than a month away and I was stuck for words. So I was thinking, hard, and quite honestly I was going around in circles in my head when Grace piped up from the backseat. "Mommy, want to hear the song I learned today in music class?" "Sure," I said, thinking that singing would keep her occupied and I could keep on working in my head. From behind me Grace's voice rose clear and lovely, filling the car:

Gonna ride up in the chariot,
Soon-a in the mornin',
Ride up in the chariot,
Soon-a in the mornin',
Ride up in the chariot,
Soon-a in the mornin',
And I hope I'll join the band.

O, Lord, have mercy on me,
O, Lord, have mercy on me,
O, Lord, have mercy on me,
And I hope I'll join the band.

Gonna meet my brother there, yes,
Soon-a in the mornin',
Meet my brother there, yes,
Soon-a in the mornin',
Meet my brother there, yes,
Soon-a in the mornin',
And I hope I'll join the band.

O, Lord, have mercy on me,
O, Lord, have mercy on me,
O, Lord, have mercy on me,
And I hope I'll join the band.

Gonna chatter with the angels,
Soon-a in the morning',
Chatter with the angels,
Soon-a in the mornin',
Chatter with the angels,
Soon-a in the mornin',
And I hope I'll join the band.

I was moved to tears. The song was a gift. It gave voice to the sense of purpose I felt but had no words to express. This is what I want, I thought. I want my colleagues and the tutors with whom I work to join the band: to gather in solidarity, with joy and determination, with intentionality, openness, and mind*full*ness in the struggle against racism. I want for us all, together, to recognize the degree to which this struggle is already ongoing all around us in our everyday lives. As scholars of composition and rhetoric, as writers and teachers of writing, and, like it or not, as functionaries, gosh darn it, within institutions that, intentionally or not, are still implicated in the unequal and unjust organization of all of our lives along racial lines. I want *us* to join the band.

Now, I am as well schooled in skepticism as any academic. During moments like these when I find myself quite suddenly and unexpectedly overcome by the onrush of emotion, I begin to feel also some concatenation of shame and, frankly, wonder at my own susceptibility. I am not typically a joiner. I value my privacy and my independence. But as I thought more about Grace's song and my response to it, including my sense of shame at being so moved by it, I realized there might be something more than weakness in my tears and something more than privacy and independence at stake in my resistance.

There are few matters in life about which I possess any degree of certainty, but this much I know, both as a matter of life experience and as a result of my studies: racism splits us, slices us apart from one another, from our humanity, even from ourselves. Racism chains us to small, crabbed notions of self, demanding of us a simultaneous denial of relations between self and Other and dependence upon those relations for a sense not only of our own existence, but also and more especially for our sense of worth. Racism distresses memory so that those multitudes who came before us, whose labors for domination or for justice are woven into the tapestry of our lives, are remembered in shreds and tatters. Or metonymically, their collective contributions are woven into singular figures: reduced to the exceptional and heroic actions of individuals, as Martin Luther King, for example, has been made to stand for a generation of civil rights activists, and George Wallace and Barry Goldwater have come to stand for generations of belief in, and careful conservation of, white entitlement. Racism constrains our imagination, limiting our ability to recognize, in both everyday and extraordinary moments, future possibility, or limiting our ability to acknowledge our individual and collective responsibility to those who will come after us—not only to our own kith and kin, but to the many generations who may follow ours. Racism binds us to a small here and a short now, making each of us, making all of us, less than what we are and less than what we might be.

In his essay "Prisoners of Hope," Cornel West wonders, "How can we be realistic about what this nation is about and still sustain hope, acknowledging that we're up against so much (2005).

Join the Band, offered so easily and simply by my daughter, moved me because it reminded me that none of us are ever alone in our struggles for racial justice and equality. To the extent that we participate in such struggles, we join a long and proud history of peoples—a band—representing many races and many faiths who have come before us. The song reminded me that there is no shame in joining when working together in common cause sustains the possibility of an end to oppression and keeps hope alive. And the song reminded me that hope is not a sign of weakness, but a necessary condition for justice struggles, for antiracist activism. This hope, as West points out, is distinct both from utopianism and optimism. The former, he suggests, substitutes vague promises of better tomorrows for the ethical, political, rhetorical work of justice struggles. The latter—optimism—West notes, "adopts the role of the spectator who surveys the evidence in order to infer that things are going to get better." "Yet we know," he writes, "that the evidence does not look good." "Hope," West continues, "enacts the stance of the participant who actively struggles against the evidence in order to change the deadly tides of wealth inequality, group xenophobia, and personal despair." Hope is not contingent upon an avoidance of the materiality, the lived realities of racism, but upon recognition, acknowledgment, and resistance to those realities. Hope demands participation, requires of us that we join.

Spirituals composed and sung by slaves sustained the hope that fueled resistance in multiple ways. Written in language and music intelligible to slaveholders as rehearsals of a Christianity that seemed to them to justify slavery, slave spirituals gave voice to a radical Christianity, to a profound faith that oppression was not, in fact, the will of God and that freedom was not an abstraction, not a dream only to be realized after death, but a potential lived reality that God willed the achievement of in this world. Just as importantly—or perhaps more so—the words of spirituals offered instruction to resisting slaves, deeply coded to be sure, on how to escape, where to find support along the way, and how to keep hope alive until escape might be possible.

Songs like *Join the Band* occupy a unique place in our collective history of racial oppression. They are not, in fact, *merely* hymns. Such songs are indeed expressions of faith, but they are also anthems of resistance. They not only evoke a historical moment during which the enslavement of African American men, women, and children was authorized by law and openly legitimated by racial ideologies of white supremacy, but also the hopeful struggle for racial justice by African Americans and, indeed, by all peoples of color. They are all-at-once articulations of belief and strategy informed by an exceptionally studied understanding of the states of mind of white captors and their henchmen, and of a sustaining belief in the possibility of realizing a world barely imaginable given the lived experience of enslavement.

In this sense, perhaps, spirituals like *Join the Band* exemplify ways of knowing and rhetorics that are integral to the antiracism movement. Antiracist discourses are akin to what James Gee terms a powerful literacy: a "meta-discourse" capable of analyzing and critiquing other discourses, including dominant discourses (2001, 542).

Antiracist discourses engage critically racial ideologies as well as the material effects of those ideologies on the lives of peoples of color as well as whites. From constructions of *rationality* to what passes for *common sense*, antiracist discourses aim at naming, resisting, countering, and transforming the everyday force of racism. Antiracist discourses are frequently tricky, taking up familiar ideas, practices, tropes, even genres, and turning them to counterpurposes, thereby exposing and exploiting their internal contradictions or reclaiming principles or spiritual traditions from their imbrication within racist systems of thought and belief.

So it is that a song like *Join the Band* might play on and with the imaginary figure of the angel—bewinged, celestial, white—and the state of being angelic, achievable only after death, transforming that figure into an earthly freedom fighter and heaven itself into a metaphor for freedom: for the possibility of fully realized humanity in the throwing off of enslavement and oppression. Without necessarily rejecting the promise of spiritual redemption familiar to the American Christians, *Join the Band*, in an antiracist context, plays with that promise, turning it from a "someday, for me, the reward of an infinity of peace" to a "today, for us, through collective struggle: freedom" vision of possibility. And it is this latter vision that moved me on that day and that continues to call to me.

While thinking about the work of antiracism as a *calling* may be uncomfortable for some of us, invoking as it does faith traditions with and against which many of us have wrestled, the term and its historical and spiritual implications have enormous significance to the antiracism movement. The work of antiracism has never been *merely* intellectual, has never been *only* pedagogical, has never depended *exclusively* on rationality, on logos, on the well-constructed argument as whites, in the Western European tradition, have historically conceived of argument. Rather, this work has taken up those *tools*, transforming them by means of allusion and metaphor, ethos and pathos, memory and history, laughter and mourning, as well as, necessarily, multiple faith traditions. Antiracist epistemologies and rhetorics are shaped variously by principle and belief as well as by a kind of fierce analytic and critical intellectual engagement or struggle with the logics of domination and oppression.

Consider, for a moment, the refusal of the Sioux nation to accept "compensation" from the federal government for the theft of the Black Hills. Briefly, in 1851, multiple tribes, including the Cheyenne, the Lakota, the Crow, and the Arikara, gathered and framed a collective agreement that the Black Hills would never be open to white settlement. This agreement— enacted according to the spiritual traditions of the tribes—was firm. In 1868, the U.S. government coerced representatives of the Sioux nation into signing the Treaty of Fort Laramie, which defined an area of land, including the Black Hills, as the Great Sioux Reservation. In 1877, following the [white] discovery of gold in the Hills, however, and a subsequent inrush of white fortune seekers, the government reneged on its treaty obligations with the Sioux, forcing them out of the Hills and into more arid and desolate lands that were less desirable—unlivable even—from a white perspective. More than one hundred years later, the U.S. Supreme Court determined that the seizure of the Hills had been illegal. Rather than returning the land, however, the Court ordered that the Sioux be compensated for their loss in the amount of $106 million (the initial price offered by the government to the Sioux, but refused by them). The Sioux Nation has steadfastly refused to accept payment for the Hills, and the money set aside by the Supreme Court for their purchase lies in investment accounts now valued at over a billion dollars.

The refusal of the Sioux to accept payment for the Black Hills might be perceived, from a traditional, white, Western political and economic perspective—shaped by convictions about the criticality of the right here and right now—as supremely irrational. Those who live on the reservations of the Sioux labor under the yoke of extreme poverty with the highest unemployment rates in the United States and with mortality rates that rival those of the poorest Third World nations. And yet by a similar measure, shifted only by longer, deeper view of time, the refusal of the Sioux suggests a wickedly astute reading of the conditions surrounding and shaping their removal from traditional lands, of treaty language, of U.S. and international law, and of the economies of the reservations. Distributed among tribal members, the current settlement amounts to little more than $10,000 per person (barely enough to purchase a good used car) and held collectively for the members is not enough to make any meaningful impact on the economic realities of reservation life. But the refusal to accept payment for the Black Hills exceeds economic reasoning. To cede the Hills to the federal government is to also, in some sense, cede sovereignty—to accede not only to the theft of what the government and white landowners might frame as property, but also to the theft of the people's right to self-determination.

And yet there is more to the refusal than those forms of reasoning that might be intelligible within and legitimated by what passes under Western eyes as rationality, as economic or political reasoning. The refusal to accept payment for the Black Hills is always also an act of principle and of belief. The Sioux are of the Hills, belong to the Hills as the Hills belong to and are of the Sioux. To sever this relation, however symbolically, given what passes for economic and political realities—to sever the Hills and the people from one another might be to break faith with a history that extends in all directions beyond the figures who stand in the Western historical imagination for the band (Crazy Horse, Sitting Bull, Big Foot, for example). To sever the Hills and the people from one another might be to break faith with a past beyond what Western thought can conceive of as memory. To sever the Hills and the people from one another might be to break a spiritual trust that overflows the limits of Western rationality and spirituality. To recognize the validity of Sioux resistance and to join in solidarity with the historical will of the Sioux Nation, those of us who are not Sioux must open ourselves to critical arguments that are familiar in form, even if they must be turned against institutions and systems upon which we have relied and in whose just design we have been taught to trust. But we may also need to open ourselves to ways of knowing and coming to know the world, to ways of understanding and animating human relations to and within the world, that exceed and transgress the certainties to which we may cling.

To speak or write of antiracist epistemologies and rhetorics requires that one speak or write also of ethics, and more than this, of ethos, just as to speak or write of racism one must also speak or write of morality. The distinction here between ethics and morality is critical. For systems of morality, as philosopher Avishai Margalit argues, are composed of those principles and rules governing behavior or treatment among groups connected to one another only by virtue of being human (or alive, in the case of our treatment of living things on and of the earth). Morality governs our thin relations, guarding us, and others, not so much against evil as against insouciance: against the cold and stark reality that we do not care equally about everyone. Ethics govern our relations with those about whom we do care, our intimates, those who compose our thick relations (2002, 37). Within the context of an antiracism movement, at some level of struggle, it matters little whether you or I or anyone *cares*, so long as systems and institutions change. The antiracism movement might be driven not so much by humanistic aims as by material ones. However, beneath this cold, hard shear of pragmatism lies another and perhaps countervailing possibility: that in the absence of care, nothing beyond the now, and maybe even nothing at all, changes.

To learn, to think, to experience, to know the world, and to speak and write as an antiracist activist, demands, I think, a copious mind, to cop a phrase from Robert Grudin, and a commodious language, to cop one from James Corder. Copia—or copious thinking—engages the thinker (and the rhetor) in the fluid interplay between and interdependence of the known and unknown, of reason and unreason, thought and feeling, critical acumen and insight, memory and hope. Copious thinking, notes Grudin, "is reason's effort to transcend its own laws, to explore and frolic beyond itself" (1997, 47). Commodious language creates worlds replete with space and time *for* difference—language that seeks not to resolve, dissolve, or suppress difference, nor yet to promote tolerance, but language that "stretch[es] words out beyond our private universe[s]" into the in-between, the place and time, history and future—into the stories that unfold at the site of conjoinment between self and Other (17).

Now, sometimes antiracist activism looks and feels far more confrontational than the above might suggest. Sometimes antiracism really is about laying down the smack, as it were. And sometimes laying down the smack is followed by the quick, sharp step in (rhetorically speaking) to force an opponent to step back. But always, I want to say, such moves are accompanied by concerted study of their effects as well as by a long lean into both the opponent and the fray to see oneself reflected there, to hear one's own voice echoing across that field of struggle. That is, there is no antiracism without deliberation, without reflection, without self-examination and critique. There is no antiracism absent the ongoing process of learning, failing, learning more and differently, and trying again. Further, there can be no antiracism absent the torrent beneath—absent copious thought and commodious language, I think. For antiracism always invokes the relation, the conjoinment, even as it confronts the forces that maintain inequality and injustice at the joint. Antiracist struggle depends, not only for its effectiveness, but also for its ongoingness, upon the will, the desire, the yearning for the barely imaginable, the world not yet seen, for the One(s) from whom the razor force of racism has severed us.

Racism, by design, seeks to inculcate both conscious and unconscious inferiority in the minds of peoples of color: that—and racism points to whites—is what you can never be; that—and racism points to racial ideology, to skewed accounts of human history, civilization, progress, to false accounts of the science of human potential—is what is better than you. Concomitantly, racism, by design, coerces whites by virtue of our race to choose our people, to choose fealty or allegiance to whiteness. Racism accomplishes this work by structuring not only our conscious but also our unconscious mind through a process of negation: that—and racism points to people of color—is what you are not; that—and racism points to racial ideology, to stereotypes and tropes of racial inferiority—is what you are better than.

Although they seem self-evident, to name these differences verges on taboo. And yet, to fail to recognize and acknowledge them impedes our ability to form meaningful multiracial alliances in the struggle against racism. They are differences that emerge from a national history of the idea of race and the practices of racism. They are also differences that emerge from the very divergent ways in which we have experienced or been subjects to that history. They are differences shaped on the one hand by collective memory and on the other by a collective practice of selective memory or, perhaps more accurately, a collective amnesia. To consider these differences deeply and to attend to the lessons they might teach about how to labor for racial justice requires that we recognize scissions between our various collective and individual memories of racial history; requires that we take note of ways in which our collective and individual racial histories teach us to whom we belong or of which groups we are or may be members; requires that we account for how we are positioned or position ourselves in relation to those histories.

Even more taboo than naming the differences created by racism in the identity formation of peoples of color and of whites is naming the possibility (probability) that the nature of the antiracism work that can and must be done by peoples of color and by whites is also different. In multiracial antiracist coalitions, peoples of color and whites shoulder different kinds of responsibilities and accountabilities. My observation is that even those of us whites who are most committed to social justice struggles, who most desire to join as allies in solidarity with antiracist activist movements, whether in the classroom where we teach, the institutions within which we make our professional lives, or within our communities, are often underprepared. We are not ready.

The problem, I think, is not that we whites lack will, desire, or energy for antiracism work. Rather, we seem often to confuse will, desire, and energy for readiness. To feel this will, desire, and energy moving within us, shaping what and how we come to know and act, can make us feel mighty fine about ourselves. It is too easy for us to begin to believe that these qualities alone transform us into a better brand of white or make us somehow less white than we were or others are. We tend too often to assume our fitness for leadership even as we turn to peoples of color to teach us what the work might be and how to do it. More often than we ought, I believe, we turn to peoples of color and—disconcerted or discommoded by what we hear—judge, attempt to correct, or—so regularly as to constitute a rather nasty pattern—stomp away feeling misunderstood. Much of what we've learned to do—acknowledging our whiteness, feeling sorrow and shame for the history of American racism and the degree to which we are implicated by that history as well as by our present, apologizing for what has and continues to be done in the name of racism—may be necessary (really more for us than for peoples of color), but is not sufficient. To the extent that we think of it at all, well-intentioned whites, I believe, tend to think of readiness for antiracist activism as a static state of mastery that, once achieved, sets the stage for future work and need not be revisited. The problem is not so much that we whites fail in the work of antiracism as a result of underpreparedness. Failures, I think, are inevitable. The problem is that we do not yet know how to create conditions in which we might learn from our failures; thus we seem not to learn very much or at all. Instead, absent altered ways of coming to know, making meaning, and acting, we seem doomed to loop endlessly and helplessly through the same tired actions and reactions, claims and counterclaims, raising the same questions over and over and moving restlessly away from them before we've lived and lain with them, feeling out the contours of the space, time, and perspectival horizons they might open for us.

And so I have set out to write a book that explores the matter of white readiness for antiracism. I have set out to write a book that digs into ways of conceiving, thinking, speaking, and acting performatively in antiracist struggles for whites. I have not undertaken this task with the misguided notion that peoples of color somehow know naturally how to do the work and therefore do not also need to learn to think anew about readiness. I do not believe, however, that it is my place to offer that instruction, nor could I offer it so well as others within the antiracism movement already do. There is a pressing need within antiracist struggles for more and better white engagement, white alliance and solidarity with peoples of color in those struggles, and for significant changes in how we whites conceive of race and racism and contend with ourselves as agents of stasis and as potential agents of change. These are the subjects I have set out to address in the pages that follow.

As a reader of academic writing, I often experience a little *frisson* of distaste when writers choose the pronoun *we*. A rhetorical conceit, I think to myself, one which, far from establishing the writer's commonality with her readers, serves instead to underscore her difference, her expertise, her superiority. As a writer, the problem of pronouns plagues me. If I choose *you*, I compose an indictment of white folks that doesn't somehow include me, when I do, in fact, mean to include myself. If I choose *I*, the pronoun might suggest to readers that they are somehow excused from considering whether or how my words might pertain to them. Alternatively, the *I* might suggest that I am offering my own perspectives and experience as easily generalizable or as an exemplar of what white perspective and experience ought to be. Perhaps I should confess that in my secret heart I wish at times I might write *they*, as in "those white people, they . . ." because I would like to be absolved of responsibility for doing whiteness—just like *them*.

Here's a moment that stopped me cold one day as I was writing this book. In the course of my reading, I came across an essay by Sara Ahmed entitled "Declarations of Whiteness: the Non-Performativity of Anti-Racism." In it, Ahmed offers up a blistering critique of whiteness studies, questioning the discourses of transcendence that so often creep into white antiracist scholarship. In part, Ahmed's critique is premised on the astute observation that there are troubling, perhaps even catastrophic, implications in what has begun to pass as a truism among antiracist scholars and activists within composition and rhetoric, as well as in other disciplines: that whiteness as a force conditioning social relations tends to be invisible and that, even more broadly, race (and racism) tend to operate as "absent presences" underwriting both scholarship and pedagogy. She writes that

it has become commonplace for whiteness to be represented as invisible, as the unseen or the unmarked, as a non-colour, the absent presence or hidden referent against which all other colours are measured as forms of deviance. But of course whiteness is only invisible for those who inhabit it. For those who don't, it is hard not to see whiteness; it even seems everywhere. Seeing whiteness is about living its effects, as effects that allow white bodies to extend into spaces that have already taken their shape, spaces in which black bodies stand out, stand apart, unless they pass, which means passing through space by passing as white. (2004, 1)

To suggest that whiteness is invisible, Ahmed notes, is to efface not only the gaze of peoples of color for whom whiteness is always already visible, but also the historical conditions, the ubiquitous and insidious racism, that make seeing whiteness necessary to the survival of peoples of color individually and collectively.

Further, Ahmed suggests that the declaration that whiteness must be seen can too easily "convert into a declaration of not being subject to whiteness or even a white subject ('if I see whiteness, then I am not white, as whites don't see their whiteness')." "Perhaps," she continues, "this fantasy of transcendence is the privilege afforded by whiteness" (2004, 4). Following from claims of having arrived at the point of seeing whiteness, Ahmed argues, is the (nonperformative) declaration that, in racial terms, white is a color too. Such claims, Ahmed writes, allow "the disappearance of the privilege of whiteness, or the disappearance of the vertical axis; the ways in which white bodies aren't simply placed horizontally alongside other bodies. To treat white bodies as if they were bodies alongside others is to imagine that we can undo the vertical axis of race through the declaration of alongsideness" (10). Both the notion that whiteness is invisible but must be seen, and the notion that whiteness is a color too, offer whites an escape route from the consequential address of racism by enacting white privilege even in and especially through the act of identification of whiteness as a racial category fundamental to the racial project of maintaining and reproducing systemic and institutional racism.

Similarly, Ahmed points out the nonperformativity of confessions to racism by white scholars and antiracist activists. Such admissions, Ahmed argues, are mired in paradox; that is, from Ahmed's perspective, too often "saying 'we are racist' becomes a claim to have overcome the conditions (unseen racism) that require the speech act in the first place. The logic goes: we say 'we are racist' and insofar as we can admit to being racist (and racists are unwitting), then we are showing that 'we are not racist', or at least that we are not racist in the same way" (2004, 5). As with the claim that whiteness must be seen, confessions of racism offer up to whites, Ahmed suggests, a fantasy of transcendence, a kind of easy way out of accountability for the differing, yet intimately connected, historical realities and lived experiences of peoples of color and whites under unjust and unequal racial orders—for racism. Expressions of shame for racism, Ahmed argues, are also fantastical—positing implicitly at least that to be sorry undoes the thing about which one feels shame and thus makes matters better or right. In fact, Ahmed suggests, declarations of shame, to the extent that they *do* anything, reposition "the white subject . . . as the social ideal" (7). Ahmed argues that public expressions of shame paradoxically enable whites to transform, through the act of apology, expressions of guilt into a reconstituted experience of pride.

Ahmed takes to task even the most radical work in whiteness studies for its reluctance to make whites feel badly about being white. Ahmed argues that white antiracism has become a mechanism for "generating a positive white identity, an identity that makes the white subject feel good about itself" (2004, 8). She goes on to suggest that "bad feelings of racism (hatred, fear, pain) are projected onto the bodies of unhappy racist whites, which allows progressive whites to be happy with themselves in the face of continued racism toward non-white others" (8).

I read Sara Ahmed's words and I stopped writing. For months.

I had been infected by the same kind of sick hopelessness that attended my reading of Elspeth Stuckey's extraordinary book, *The Violence of Literacy* (1990). The issue for me in the case of both readings was not that Ahmed or Stuckey was wrong, but the possibility that each of them had had the last word— that there was nothing left to say. After a first reading neither analysis seemed to me to leave any opening, any crack of space through which any theory of productive agency or of change might enter.

For a time, I mourned.

Perhaps, I worried, there is simply nothing to be done, no means by which the struggle against racism might be effectively joined by whites, or at least no means by which the struggles of peoples of color and whites against racism might be conjoined.

Then one morning I woke up angry. At myself, really. For my own capacity to slip away, to find an excuse not to engage.

Ahmed's argument does not obviate the necessity of (re) membering white racial experience and giving voice to those stories in successive drafts in order to both learn to tell them and learn how to tell them mindfully and meaningfully. Her work might suggest, however, that this kind of learning in action is the work of making oneself ready for antiracist activism; that this kind of learning in action is necessary, integral even, to the possibility of whites ever realizing a performative antiracism— but that it is always insufficient. In fact, there is and will be nothing but insufficiency until the idea of race, itself, is eradicated and with it our ideas of whiteness itself. White antiracism must of historical necessity be enacted within paradoxical conditions. Racism is an effect of thinking racially, and we can't resist racism without also thinking racially. We have to name, engage with, and resist the concept of race and the ideological and material conditions of racial formation even though to do so is to invoke the (ir)rationality of race itself. For neither the idea of race nor the practice of racism can be willed away by not thinking about them. From the crucible of Western thought, social organization, and political economies, we whites have formed a racial hegemony to which there is no readily apparent exterior.

Ahmed's work might suggest to all of us white folks a set of difficult, complex, and extraordinarily uncomfortable possibilities:

that the work of critiquing whiteness from the inside (whites studying whiteness) is always necessary, always inadequate, always more integral and critical to the ongoing learning of whites than of peoples of color. Such critique is only useful to the extent that whites are able to (a) learn to think, feel, and do differently and resistingly as a result of their critique and (b) recognize in an ongoing and enlarging sense that the work of white antiracism cannot be altruistic and still be antiracist. That is, whites must recognize in an ongoing and enlarging sense the extent to which the humanity of those of us who are raced white depends upon our learning to be conscious as well as critical of and resistant to racial states of thinking, organizing, being, and doing. And, of course, we must care more about our humanity than about the preservation of our whiteness and our attachments to our reputations as *good* people in our own eyes as well as in the eyes of peoples of color.

Ahmed's work, in the great tradition of Audre Lorde and bell hooks, Gloria Anzuldúa, Patricia Williams, and more women of color than I can reasonably name, demands response rather than silence. I ought, I realized (we ought, I realized) to recognize in her work the kind of challenge that white antiracists should, must, can take up—seeking not to dismiss or negate what has been said, but to recognize the gift in the critique. We might choose to lean in, to stay for a time listening, and to hear, finally, the invitation to press on with the challenge, the critique in mind—beyond the staid and overstated, beyond the endless loop of mindless failures and the infinite reiterations of questions we've no intention of resolving, to points more unfamiliar, more strange, and perhaps more promising.

So, I started writing again, and because I was writing, I was also thinking again. *I Hope I Join the Band*, which is the result of that writing and thinking and writing some more, does not offer comfort or ease. Instead, the book essays into the complexity of imagining worlds not yet seen, labors not yet accomplished, tentative understandings at the threshold between self and Other. Rather than abjuring the affective (in this case, spiritual and emotional) dimensions of antiracism work for whites as well as for peoples of color and eliding the intimate relations between praxis and poesis, *I Hope I Join the Band* experiments with (re)articulating their conjunctures in the context of antiracist epistemologies and rhetorics.

Joining the band is not so easy as simply invoking a beautiful old spiritual, not so easy as desiring or even needing to join. And to merely exhort folks to join is to dishonor, I think, the memory of those who have truly given over their lives to the struggle for racial justice. The real question, especially for whites, given what are undeniably patterns of white abdication in the antiracism movement, is *how* to join and *keep on* joining intelligently, responsibly, mindfully. In part—and here's a hard reality—joining is difficult because there is no *imaginable* end to the struggle nor a perfectly complete answer to the question of how to carry on the struggle. Our past accretes in our present and we carry it with us even as we attempt to imagine future possibilities. We cannot, I believe, *un*think the idea of race. We can't undo the historical tapestry of injustice and oppression that the idea of race has woven. Trying to forget that history, as we've seen or should be able to see, has enabled only the perpetuation of racism in a range of vicious forms, from the most overtly violent and explicit, to the most coded and subversive.

There could easily be, I recognize, the kind of satisfying suck of sound-bite experience to the phrase *join the band.* We could latch onto the words and happily, *mindlessly,* assert them. But the inevitable (and righteous) critiques that would follow from that latching on might well lead us to discard any praxis (or poesis) we might conceive before we've actually explored the phrase's complexity and significance. And the accumulation of certainty that we cannot construct, in a series of predictable and assessable steps rationally derived, a means to the end of racism might continue to sustain our collective attention deficit disorder when it comes to fighting racism, justifying our sense of hopelessness, and helping to maintain the consensual relation between us and what we know (or at least are willing to say we know) to be an unjust racial order.

I Hope I Join the Band begins in the nexus of activism and scholarship, taking as its starting point an idea central to community-based antiracist education and leadership development that first became evident to me as I began my own formal training as an antiracism activist in the mid-1990s in Albany, New York. That is, neither the why nor the how of antiracism conceived as praxis (as philosophy and practice) is self-evident. If as activists and scholars, rhetors and teachers, we are to engage in the work of antiracism to create institutions and communities, classrooms and writing centers, that are loci for antiracist work, we will have to acknowledge that we have a lot to learn. We need to study hard; we need to try and fail and learn from our failures; and we need to recognize and live with the recognition that there will be no end to the necessity for this learning: there will be no epiphany, no singular moment in which we know, finally and forever, everything we need to know. And finally, we will not learn everything we need to know from books; much of what we learn we will be taught by one another, by getting lost in memory and in story, by risking our selves as we give voice to our lostness, and, probably, by chance or accident as well. To learn in this way will require that we are prepared, are ready to learn in ways for which no amount of graduate school may prepare us. *I Hope I Join the Band* is about the cultivation of this active and emerging state of readiness.

A LITTLE HISTORY, A LITTLE CONTEXT

Perhaps it is not necessary to rehearse once more an expansive history of race and racism in the United States for the purposes of this book. But it may be useful to remember through a few broad strokes the character of that past in order to discern how racism continues to function and why antiracist activism might be an appropriate praxis for those of us concerned with social justice. For a brief time following the end of the Civil War, it seemed to some that the United States might fulfill its philosophical promise with the realization of a multiracial democracy. But ideologies of race, and of white supremacy in particular, were more powerful, more pervasive, than was the collective will toward that realization and, moreover, were cut through with a perceived need for cheap labor and land. Racism and an unmitigated belief in white supremacy shaped popular narratives about the chaos and complexity of postwar America, justifying and legitimating the reclamation of white power through the enactment of Jim Crow laws, the continuation of the virtual extirpation of American Indian peoples, and the racialization, exclusion, and oppression of immigrants from many lands to the United States. By 1910, Jim Crow laws were firmly in place, and a racial order that insured the continued domination by whites of peoples of color was fully restored and guaranteed, as it were, through the protections of the state.

Resistance to systemic racism and to white supremacist ideology was ongoing during this period as, indeed, it had been prior to the Civil War.[1] Organized resistance began most famously and, arguably, most effectively in the 1950s as peoples of color organized around the Supreme Court's landmark *Brown vs. Board* decision. This decision was rather quickly followed by other landmark moments, including the Civil Rights Act of 1964, banning discrimination on the basis of race in employment and public spaces; the Voting Rights Act of 1965; the Immigration and Nationality Services Act of 1966, which opened up the United States to immigration from countries outside of Europe; and the Civil Rights Act of 1968, which banned racial discrimination in housing. But even as these pieces of legislation became the law of the land, men and women who had struggled for civil rights were realizing that ideologies of race, racism, and white supremacy seemed impervious to the law.[2] In the everyday, lived

---

1. For a wonderful history of antiracism in the United States, see Herbert Aptheker's book *Anti-Racism in U.S. History: the First Two Hundred Years.*

2. For a fuller explication of the slipping of racial ideology and racism under and through the law, see Derrick Bell's work, especially *And We Are Not Saved: The Elusive Quest for Racial Justice.*

experience of peoples of color, despite the law, racism continued, shifting, changing shape, morphing into new and equally
or increasingly insidious forms as it exceeded the capacity of
the law to contain or mitigate its effects. Although the history
of the civil rights era is frequently offered up with a markedly
triumphalist spirit, and although the changes enacted in that
era were significant, ideologies of race and white supremacy, as
well as racism, survived, not unchallenged but still powerful and
vicious in spite of and perhaps because of their coding within
social, political, and economic narratives of individual successes
and collective failures.

The modern antiracism movement in the United States is, in
the first instance, rooted in traditions of community and labor
organizing and driven by a recognition that racism is not a
thing of the past but a divisive and destructive force, living and
reproducing within and through systems and institutions that
shape the public and private lives of us all. Perhaps most nota-
ble among the modern or post-civil-rights movement antiracist
organizations is the People's Institute for Survival and Beyond,
founded in 1980 by Ron Chisom (Louisiana) and Jim Dunn
(Ohio). The institute provides antiracist education, leadership
training, and organizing support to community activists committed to antiracism. There has long been and continues to be
a symbiotic relationship between the antiracism activist movement and the evolution of academic antiracism in the form of
a growing body of scholarship in critical race studies and race
theory across a range of disciplines, including rhetoric and
composition. The community antiracism movement takes up
and uses histories and theories composed within academia in
its preparation of antiracist community leaders. Scholars draw
from their own and others' experiences as antiracist activists in
order to better understand, analyze, and theorize the dynamics
of racialization and everyday enactments of racism and white
supremacy writ large and small—within systems, institutions,
and across communities.

Antiracist activists and scholars do not all think alike. Within the antiracism movement there are fracture lines and splinter groups; practical disagreements about how to organize, how to act effectively and productively, how to prioritize actions; and philosophical disagreements about how power circulates and how change occurs or even to what extent change might occur. There are disagreements about who should do what work within the movement—about the roles of peoples of color and whites and how multiracial coalitions can be formed and sustained over time.

The one relative constant, however, within the network of antiracist scholars and activists is this: generally speaking, we agree that there is sufficient evidence across a wide range of social, political, and economic contexts within the United States, and accessible for study across a wide range of disciplines, to conclude that while race may be a social construct, race matters, and racism (whether one conceives of it in individual, institutional, or systemic terms or all of the above) is real—has material effects that work to privilege whites and to disadvantage, marginalize, or exclude peoples of color. This doesn't mean that we don't spend time collecting, sifting, weighing information or data. It doesn't mean that we assume the meaning or significance of evidence. But it does mean that the questions that animate antiracist scholarship tend not to circulate around whether racism is real, but around how to understand racism conceptually and practically, why racism works as it does and against whom, and how and why racism advantages and disadvantages and in what ways. Our questions range from the historical, to the analytical, theoretical, and critical, to the pragmatic—what to do, how to do it, and why do it in the right-here-right-now.

Within the field of composition, rhetoric, and writing-center studies, interest and investment in race-critical studies and antiracist pedagogy is running high. Further, in what are, by any measure, deeply troubled times,[3] our field is experiencing

---

3. For example, the Southern Poverty Law Center reports a 244% increase in the numbers of "patriot" groups in 2009, including the formation of forty-

a renewed commitment and sense of urgency toward activism as a legitimate and critical aspect of our work as scholars, but also and perhaps more especially as teachers and tutors of writing. In Houston, at the 2007 International Writing Centers Association Conference, the first IWCA Anti-Racism Special Interest Group drew roughly ten attendees. By gathering time at the 2009 International Writing Centers Association Conference held in Las Vegas, Nevada, over fifty writing-center tutors and directors crowded into a meeting room for the SIG. Similarly, of the eleven featured sessions at the 2010 Conference on College Composition and Communication, six included panelists speaking specifically and centrally about race. Following the 2007 publication of my essay, *Beyond the Known: Writing Centers and the Work of Anti-Racism* in the *Writing Center Journal,* I have been asked to give keynote addresses at two national conferences a plenary address at the Midwest Writing Centers Association Conference, and numerous talks and workshops for composition and rhetoric faculty and writing-center consultants at universities across the Midwest. At each of these engagements I have been struck by the intensity of need and desire expressed by participants for deeper understanding of American conceptions of race and racism, for more principled and concrete ways of knowing, being, and doing in resistance to racism, and for deeper, more sustained multiracial dialogues about race and racism.

As hopeful and as promising as our field's current investment in a deeper understanding of race and racism seems, the disagreements that agitate the antiracist activist movement

---

two new militia groups. On March 20, 2010, The Hill, a political blog, as well as the *Huffington Post* and other news sources, reported that Representative Andre Carson and Representative John Lewis (a hero of the civil rights movement) had been called the n-word by "tea party" protesters at the U.S. Capitol; the crowd spit upon another black lawmaker. Not coincidently, on the same day, Representative Barney Frank was called a faggot by protesters. And, on April 23, 2010, Arizona's governor, Jan Brewer, signed into state law anti-immigration legislation making the failure to carry proof of citizenship a crime and requiring law enforcement officials to detain anyone unable to document their citizenship.

are also at work here. Race and racism are frequently subordi-
nated within the discourses of the discipline and its subfields to
"broader" tropes such as "culture" or "identity." At some level,
this subordination is an understandable enactment of a legitimate interest within the field in examining the ways in which
multiple identities intersect and overlap, magnifying or mitigat-
ing particular forms of privilege and marginalization or oppression. But the subordination of race and racism within broader
conversations about "culture" or "identity" has had a number of
deleterious effects. Racial ideologies, the codification of those
ideologies in law, and the systemization of those ideologies in
and through American institutions (beginning with the contradiction between the constitutional claim of equality and the
simultaneous preservation of slavery for the purposes of political expediency, at least) distinguish American racial ideologies and American racism from global conceptions of race and
enactments of racism. While some of the history of race and
racism in the United States does intersect with or inform and
influence ideologies and enactments elsewhere in the world,
the subordination of race and racism to "culture" or "identity"
agitates against a studied engagement with the historical specificity of American racial ideology and American racism.

Further, this subordination enables rather than intervenes in
the assertion of easy and largely inaccurate analogies between
the lived experiences of peoples of color with racism and the
lived experiences of those of us who occupy other marginalized
or oppressed subject positions. The experience of being subject
to sexism, for example, does not teach me everything I need to
know about the experience of being subject to racism. While I
do not wish to argue that one form of oppression is worse than
all the rest, I do want to assert that racism has a particular historical specificity and social weight within the United States
that is significantly different from other forms of oppression.
Let us admit that the idea of race is so thoroughly discredited
as to be absurd. But let us also admit and not disguise the fact
that the material conditions that are the effects of systemic and

institutional racism are real. To understand those conditions, to learn to recognize and dismantle them, we must stay with race and racism for a little while longer.

In the academy as in public discourse, antiracist activists are often called upon to engage with questions or challenges that, in some sense, we have moved beyond in our scholarship. The subordination of race and racism to "culture" or "identity" enables all of us to slip away when conversations about race and racism get hard. Across a wide array of contexts, from the community meeting or legislative hearing to the department meeting or the classroom, we face the challenge of defining, in what can feel like endless (re)iterations, racism as a *rhetorical exigency*: as a problem, crisis, or dilemma that can and must be addressed through discourse. Further and relatedly, we face the challenge of asserting the materiality of racism within a social context in which the possibility of "plausible" deniability at systemic, institutional, and individual levels is maintained by a web of historical, economic, and political hegemonies animated by race and sustained or legitimated by ongoing dynamic and fluid, but persistent, racial ideologies. Terribly and often tragically, however legitimate our certainties may be, our assertions of them, whether as community activists, scholars, or teachers, seem to be least effective rhetorically speaking. We do not succeed or even move productively very often when our rhetorical means depend upon the persuasiveness of what we know for sure: on historical, sociological, economic, or political evidence in the "objective" sense, or on the ethical imperative to exercise our agency in service of racial justice.

Both from the Right and from the Left, we are stymied, I think, in talking well with one another about race and racism, by intransigent beliefs in our own goodness as well as by our conviction—our need, perhaps, to believe—that such talk is useless. Instantiations of racism ranging from the most overt articulations of racial ideology to the "silent racism" of white progressives are shaped by these beliefs. And belief, as James Carse writes, "has a confrontational element built into itself that is essential to its own vitality. If believers need to inspire fellow believers to hold firmly to their positions, they need just as much to inspire nonbelievers to hold to theirs" (Carse, 2009, "Belief"). Racial ideology concatenates the self and the social so that to speak of one is to invoke the other. In this context, to appeal or exhort with certainty alone seems too often to involve constructing a stance of rhetorical innocence for the white speaker that distinguishes her from those to whom she appeals.

White antiracist epistemology needs to begin not with our beliefs (including our belief or the intimation of belief in our own innocence), but with our individual and collective awakening to that which we do not know, with our reach toward "the art of seeing the unknown everywhere, especially at the heart of our most emphatic certainties" (Carse 1987). And rather than eliding that which we do not know or attempting to disguise our uncertainty, white antiracist rhetoric requires a long lean into our collective ignorance and, from that place and time of unknowing, the voicing of wonder about what the world has been, is, and might be.

I Hope I Join the Band begins here—with the invitation for white activists, scholars, and teachers to stay, if only for a moment, with race and racism. Not because nothing else is important or because they are unrelated to other identities and other forms of oppression, but because race and racism do, in fact, matter differently, and they matter in ways we cannot inquire into unless and until we attend to them with the fullness of our attention—without slipping away. *I Hope I Join the Band* is a book for those who wonder how, why, and to what extent our lives as actors, as rhetors, are shaped by ideologies of race, and for those who hear the call to act: to organize and facilitate, to study, write, and teach with both will and readiness for hopeful resistance.

2

CHATTERING WITH ANGELS

"I wonder," says my colleague, "if I could ask you a question." We are sitting in a restaurant booth in the Midwest. I've been invited here to offer a workshop on antiracism. Our conversation had wound slowly to this moment, my colleague telling me a little of her childhood, her experience of being a light-skinned Latina woman in a family that prized light skin ever so highly; about a father who hated Mexicans, who maybe hated himself. About her children and their schools. About her work at the university. "I wonder if I could ask you a question? I think the workshop participants may want to know. Actually, I imagine everybody who meets you wants to know." I can see she is nervous, but I think I know the question already. I smile. I invite her to ask.

"Who are you? I mean," she hesitates, trying perhaps to make the question smoother, "why do you do this work? Why do you care?" She apologizes immediately. Maybe she asked too bluntly, she worries. But I think it's a fair question for a person of color to ask of a white woman coming to town to lead an antiracism workshop and perhaps also a fair question for readers to ask of a white woman writing a book about antiracism. Who are you? This is a question that deserves a thoughtful answer and as true an answer as one can offer in the moment it is asked. I am qualifying the term *true*, and here's why: the preservation and conservation of white identity depends upon a very particular answer to the question *who are you?* It depends upon the answer *not you.* But white identity may also be preserved by answering in denial mode: "Why, I'm just like you." Or in obsequious mode: "I'm not you, but I'm on your side." Or in refusal mode writ cute: "I'm nobody, who are you?" Or more pointedly: "Isn't it obvious? Why would you even need to ask that question?"

In some way, I think, anyone who is asked the question *who are you?* must answer provisionally. We are all, as Judith Butler would say, opaque to some degree, even, and perhaps especially, to ourselves. For Butler, it is our recognition of our opacity to ourselves that might enjoin us to interest in and openness to the incompleteness, the tentativeness, the ongoingness of one another's answers to a question like *"who are you?"* (2005, 136). And yet, with particular regard to raced-white identity, there are matters beyond the opacity of which Butler speaks that impede one's ability to both attend to the question and answer truly and provisionally. For we whites are taught carefully and from birth the art of selective forgetfulness. We are taught also, alongside the mastery of spoon and fork, of high fives and the first articulations of words, that who we are as raced subjects is not a matter requiring too much thought on the one hand, but demanding the cultivation of very particular forms of consciousness on the other. Whiteness is all-at-once a story that need never be told and a story that is endlessly replicating, endlessly asserted through successive denials.

Who are you? My colleague has asked me for a story and it's a righteous request. Of course, I can't tell all of it, can't get it all in, get it all right, but I can give a story as true as I can make it by telling who I think I am today.

The stony gray edifice of the church, St. Peter Clavier, sits high on a bluff just off the interstate, in St. Paul, Minnesota. In the early spring, with the trees still devoid of leaves and the sand in the church playground a soup of mud and leaves and twigs, the place looks forlorn. My husband parks the car and we join the stream of congregants walking to the doors, our children, Dan and Lucy, clinging to our hands and looking about wide eyed and curious. I walk carefully, awkwardly. I'm very pregnant. We've come at the invitation of Sister Mary Lou, my favorite of Mike's many aunts. Sister Mary Lou has told me that I will like this church. It's a church wherein a real multitude gather, not effectively segregated like the other churches we've attended with Mike's family. Its priest preaches a liberation theology and the congregants, she says, come to celebrate, truly, the promise of liberation. In the pew, my little boy on one side and Sister Mary Lou on the other, I look and listen and smile wryly at my husband as we stand up, sit down, kneel, sit, then stand again. A father in the row ahead of us towers above the rest. His back is broad and he stands so straight and tall. Resting on his shoulder and gazing back at me is a baby girl. Her skin is glowing, chocolaty brown, and her huge, round, brown eyes are shining. Her hair is a halo of black ringlets. I grin at her. She's beautiful, I think. She stares back, unblinking. I grin some more and a gummy baby smile begins to emerge. We sit once more, and in a quiet moment my son turns to me and asks in a worried, nearly horrified voice, "Mommy, will our little baby look like us?"

A wave of mortification washes over me. I offer up a silent prayer of thanks for Sister Mary Lou's hearing aids, which don't always work that well. But I think I've seen the muscles of the father's back tighten just for a moment. He shifts the baby from his shoulder to his lap so I can no longer see her. What troubles me, I reflect, isn't that Dan has given voice for the first time to his perception of racial difference. What troubles me is that he has given voice for the first time to white supremacy: to his sense that to look like us is to look right ,and his desire for his own reflection in the skins of those with whom he will most closely affiliate—to whom he will belong and who will belong to him. I tell this story to another of Mike's aunts, who is also a favorite of mine. She laughs wildly and repeats it at every family gathering for months.

Each time the story is told, I remember. I am in a grocery store with my mother and my brother. Rick is black haired and brown eyed. His skin is nut brown, his cheekbones high, and his nose long and straight. He's tall and strong and, in our not just predominantly but overwhelmingly white hometown, he stands out like a sore thumb. Rick and I trip along behind the cart up and down the aisles. Sometimes, my mother lets my brother push the cart and me ride on the front. We laugh as he threatens to run me into a display of soup cans. My mother spots a colleague who is also shopping in the store. They stop to chat and my brother and I stand, waiting and bored. My mother's friend is tall, I remember. She looks down at us and smiles. She looks at my brother and her voice goes high and fake. "Ooooh . . . and whose little boy is this?" My mother stiffens and her voice is tense. "This is my son, Rick. And this is my daughter, Frankie." My brother stares at the woman—unflinching.

My mother's colleague, I reflect when I am ruminating on this memory, gave voice to what was really a shared sense in our community: that this nut-brown, black-haired boy did not belong. His presence in our family and within our community was an aberration, an accident that disturbed individual and collective convictions about how families, communities, even the universe, perhaps, ought to be racially ordered. Rick's presence was like an itch that white folks seemed to constantly feel the need to scratch. From my own standpoint, Rick belonged with me and I with him. Best friend, constant companion, tease, and tormentor, Rick was essential to my sense of family, of security, of being loved and loving. But I knew. I heard the discordance, the reverb produced in the collisions between the racial convictions of our white community and the fact of *us* as a family. I felt the tension and the pull to choose to belong to that community rather than to Rick. Choosing to belong and to belong to one another, and quite often failing to live that choice faithfully and well, was an everyday affair.

Who are you? The question stays with me, troubles me. In some way, to tell the story as I've told it so far is to tell you not so much who I am, but that I am not my brother, that I am different from him and that he was marked as a racial Other within our family and within our home community. By implication, I was marked as one-of-us, as belonging, and as "normal" (at least in racial terms). I've also suggested that the marking of this difference and the inequalities in recognition, in acknowledgment, in willingness to build and sustain relationship, troubled me as a child and continue to trouble me as an adult. I've suggested, in other words, that from a young age I have been conscious of a set of prevailing racial rules that govern familial relations and affiliative relationships. People who belong together, who are beloved of one another as lovers, brothers and sisters, even as friends, are supposed to look like one another. And this consciousness agitates me.

As a child, the rules rubbed painfully against the lived reality of my everyday life: against the reciprocity of love and care my brother and I felt for one another. The rules of racial standing, while serving my interests or benefiting me by establishing my status as a white girl—opening up access to social and educational opportunities for me—also broke me into pieces, sliced me away from one whom I loved dearly, passionately, crazily (in the crazy mixed-up way siblings so often do love one another). Rick and I belonged and still do belong to one another by virtue, in the most superficial sense, of our shared family history, but also by virtue of the love we felt and still feel for one another. However, let's face it, even familial love is at some level a choice; although the possibility of loving one another was forged within that family history, we chose one another too. And even though we shared a family, even though we chose one another, the racism we lived with, that shaped our lives and that we experienced differently by virtue of our races, warped our relationship. The lived realities of racialization and the effects of racism were never really invisible to me, but how to name those realities without capitulating to them, how to talk back to them—resisting the effects of racism and the ways racism twisted and contorted even the love my brother and I felt for each other—has never been self-evident to me.

In his article *Memoria Is a Friend of Ours: On the Discourse of Color*, Victor Villanueva notes that not everything that needs to be thought and said can be conceived through and spoken by academic discourse. Personal narrative is necessary and integral to the creation and sustenance of community and solidarity among and between peoples of color. "The narratives of people of color" he writes, "jog our memories as a collective in a scattered world and within an ideology that praises individualism" (2004, 16). "The personal here," he notes, "does not negate the need for the academic; it complements, provides an essential element in the rhetorical triangle, an essential element in the intellect—cognition *and* affect. The personal done well is sensorial and intellectual, complete, knowledge known throughout mind and body, even if vicariously" (14–15). Further, Villanueva continues,

> The narrative of the person of color validates. It resonates. It awakens, particularly for those of us who are in institutions where are numbers are few. WE know that though we really are Gramsci's exceptions . . . our experiences are in no sense unique but are always analogous to other experiences from among those exceptions. (14–15)

Villanueva advocates for the opening up of space within writing classrooms (and writing centers) for the composition of personal or memory narratives by students of color. He argues that writing teachers, and I'll add, by extension, writing consultants, need to learn to sustain conditions in which the conception and composition of such narratives can be taught and taught well. But Villanueva also argues, implicitly at least, that writing teachers and consultants need to prepare ourselves to participate actively and reflectively in the creation of contexts in which such narratives may be valued and learned from, not merely produced and then gawked at, as it were. We need to learn to read, to engage with one another's stories, not as voyeurs but as players, in a dramatic sense, within them, and as actors who may be changed not only by the telling of our own our stories, but also by the practices of listening, attending, acknowledging, and honoring the stories of our students and our colleagues of color as well. "Looking back," Villanueva writes, "we look ahead, and giving ourselves up to the looking back and the looking ahead, knowing the self and, critically, knowing the self in relations to others, maybe we can be an instrument whereby students can hear the call" (2004, 17).

The learning and teaching labor for which Villanueva calls in *Memoria* resonates with, and is, in part at least, constitutive of the kind of multiracial antiracist activism already ongoing in communities around the country. Those of us who are academics and who hope to join in the work of antiracism will need to stop minimizing the complexity and significance of narrative, stop depoliticizing the personal, and start studying the rich epistemological and rhetorical traditions that inform the narratives of peoples of color. Further, those of us who are white may need to admit that we have not yet begun, really, to craft epistemological and rhetorical practices or a performative antiracist narrative tradition that might enable us to join meaningfully and productively with multiracial, antiracist coalitions in doing the work of antiracism. If this is so, and if knowing how to begin and sustain this kind of work is not self-evident (and it isn't), then those of us in academia need to begin admitting that we don't know and lean into the possibility of learning. But antiracist epistemology and rhetoric are neither learned nor created under conditions of passivity or inaction. In order to learn—as this kind of learning requires experimentation—we will need to risk speaking aloud about what we are learning even before we know very much of anything with certainty. We will need to admit our limit—and indeed the limits whiteness places on us—as philosophers and rhetors.

Villanueva points to the particular necessity of memory, of poetry and of storytelling, for students and teachers of color. It's hard to imagine very many white readers encountering that claim and not wondering, at some level, *what about me?* We might laugh at our tendency to recenter ourselves when we are called to decenter; we should laugh and feel horrified as well. But in this particular case, underneath that first disturbing impulse is a worry I, at least, want to have and want to share with other whites. I want us to think, really think and feel, really feel the question of whether, to what degree, and how it might be possible for whites to join with peoples of color, as partners and allies in the creation and sustenance of antiracist communities outside of or within colleges and universities.

I suspect I'm not the only one who would like, at some level, to say "yes, of course" and move right on past the question of how. But there are, I think, the limits of *whiteliness* with which we must contend. *Whiteliness* is defined by Minnie Bruce Pratt and, later, by Marilyn Frye, as learned ways of knowing and doing characterized by a racialized (white) sense of oneself as best equipped to judge, to preach, and to suffer. "Whitely people," Frye writes, "generally consider themselves to be benevolent and good-willed, fair, honest, and ethical. . . . Whitely people have a staggering faith in their own rightness and goodness, and that of other whitely people" (2001, 90–91). Further, Frye notes, for whitely people, "Change cannot be initiated unless the moves are made in appropriate ways. The rules are often-rehearsed" (91). Problems must be presented in the *right* way in order to be processed and addressed. Whitely people conceive of themselves as appropriate arbiters of what might constitute *the right way*. And whiteliness impedes the ability of white folks to change, to be changed in and through our relationships with peoples of color and by the analyses they offer to us of the materiality of racism in all of our lives.[1]

It's a truism within much of the antiracist activist movement that peoples of color cannot reasonably be asked by whites to shoulder, alone, the burden of struggling against racism. First, it isn't fair to expect peoples of color to do all the work, particularly as, let's be honest, race is an idea that, by design, has served white interests, and as racism is a white problem. Second, so long as a preponderance of whites, wittingly or no, consent to the mindless reproduction of whiteness and the continuing unequal distribution of power and access along racial lines within American political, social, and economic systems and institutions (including education), racism will

---

1. For another excellent treatment of whiteliness see Fox (2002).

continue to flourish even as it morphs into new forms to shape our consciousness and the material conditions of all of our lives. It seems also clear that, to a large extent, the survival and thriving of communities of color continue without, and frequently in spite of, the "assistance" of either white allies or well-intentioned whites. Despite the extent to which we whites have been steeped in the whitely notion that we do know best and are best equipped to lead, very often we have been the ones who have impeded the effectiveness of antiracism struggles; our leadership, such as it is, has been misdirected, misguided, often patronizing, insulting, and tinged with racism, if not outrightly racist.[2]

In my experience, white people—no matter how well-intentioned we may be, no matter how deep our relations with peoples of color may be, no matter how much we may desire to belong with and to people of color—never get a free pass through whiteliness. Undoing this mindscape—learned from the cradle, from the first intentional reach for comfort from another being, from the first word—is an everyday, intentional, and deliberative labor. It's a real question, then, whether and how we will begin and sustain this work. Can white activists, teachers, and tutors join with colleagues of color in antiracism work? Can we participate in the creation of productive conditions within our communities, classrooms, and writing centers for peoples of color to story their lives well and meaningfully? Can we possibly learn to listen, to recognize and acknowledge, without recentering ourselves, without recentering whiteness, or at least can we learn to resist the sucking force of *whiteliness* as we attend? And is there a necessity for a different range of registers for white activists, teachers, and students to *re*-member and story our lives as raced-white subjects? What, in other words, might we need to learn before, and continue learning as, we lean into and take our first steps toward solidarity, make our first forays into the creation and enactment of antiracist activism

---

2. See, for example, Frye (2001); Ahmed (2004); Pratt et al. (1988).

and pedagogy? These are questions, I really believe, we will only answer by trying, by making the way as we move, to invoke Myles Horton. And our ability to move at all will depend on our ability to sustain humility and to recognize the ongoing necessity of being learners willing to try even though we do not, in fact, know much and may well fail.

In his book *Racism Without Racists: Color-Blind Racism and the Persistence of Racial Inequality in the United States*, Eduardo Bonilla-Silva notes the centrality of storytelling to our "presentation and representation" of "ourselves and others." Defining stories as "'social events that instruct us about social processes, social structures, and social situations,'" Bonilla-Silva suggests that in addition to helping us to construct arguments and to persuade, stories enable us to narrate status. "The stories we tell are not random," he writes. Rather, "They evince the social position of the narrators . . . storytelling often represents the most ideological moments; when we tell stories we tell them as if there was *only one way* of telling them, as the 'of course' way of understanding what is happening in the world. These are moments when we are 'least aware that [we] are using a particular framework, and that if [we] used another framework the things we are talking about would have different meaning" (2006, 75; italics in original). Bonilla-Silva's message is not, I think, that we ought not tell stories: we must. Rather, we might learn from him the necessity of becoming conscious and critical of the frameworks that shape the stories we are telling. We need to be clear about the nature of the ways of knowing we employ as storytellers and the forms of knowledge we privilege as we narrate our lives as raced-white subjects.

To tell the story of who I am as I have told it thus far might be an example of the use of pursuant ideation, which is arguably the most common story frame of raced-white narrative. Pursuant ideation is the ability to form thoughts, to imagine or conceive, proceeding from and conforming to past experience, prior knowledge, formal or informal instruction. I have described one dimension of the formation of my sense of who

I am as a raced-white subject and traced along a rather tenuous thread how it is, perhaps, that I have come to conceive of myself, to compose myself in this way. It is time to acknowledge again that any accounting of this kind will inevitably be partial and inadequate, but also now to take note of the ways in which even the partiality, the inadequacies of such accounts, may be illuminating. For I have also suggested, by implication at least, that by virtue of my relationship to my brother—my love for him and his for me—as well as by virtue of the racial consciousness I developed as a result of that relationship, I am different from, see differently than, other whites. I have implied, perhaps, that I see more or better not because one of my best friends is a person of color (which would be bad), but because my own brother is a person of color (which is worse, I think).

If white participation in the production of resisting stories of racialized experience is to be meaningful, the stories we tell and the manner of their production must be conceived of as opportunities to learn, to revise, to reconstruct in order to more fully represent, one hopes, increasingly nuanced understandings. We will need to learn the practice of excavating memories of our own racialization, but also learn to connect those memories to the crucible of history in which the idea of race was forged and the practices of racism, of white supremacy in particular, were justified, legitimated, and reproduced. Our stories will need to be less declarations of immutable truths than tremulous and vulnerable explorations of the question, what has it meant and what does it mean to be raced-white subjects? And further we will need to ask, what does it mean to live racialized subjectivities and what might it mean to resist those social locations and their effects in service of pressing back against the historical weight and force of racism and of white supremacy?

Perhaps most of all, we whites will need to learn the ways and degrees to which our stories are troubled and, perhaps, contradicted by the stories of peoples of color. We will need to be willing to revise and resubmit without an end in sight, letting go of our conviction that to tell our stories might confer transcendence of our whiteness upon us (Ahmed, 2004, 4). To tell our stories should shift us from the ground we believe we know to that which we cannot know, where error is a virtual certainty and failure might be as well. To invoke Elizabeth Boquet's conception of "high-risk/high-yield" in *Noise from the Writing Center* (2001), to pose and respond to such questions requires a willingness to risk one's *self* and to imagine the potential yield of that risk not only in terms of gain, but also in the sense of getting one's *self* out of the way.

To proceed with narrative in this way requires telling without certifying those strands of the story with which we are most comfortable, that please us in some sense, but also giving voice to those strands that discomfort, that mortify, that disrupt our sense of goodness and righteousness. To get ourselves out of the way in such an enterprise requires that we recognize the degree to which our stories of ourselves as raced-white subjects are also the stories of a people who possess a history, and that our experiences and the stories we make of them are effects of that history. This is the practice of critical ideation, signifying the ability to form thoughts, to imagine or conceive in ways that connect past experience, prior knowledge, and current lived conditions to social, political, and economic forces forged in the crucible of histories: of ideas and ideologies, of power and its exercise, of peoples and the organization of their relations. The purpose of the telling, in this context, can never be the achievement of absolution or of transcendence, but the excavation and critical examination of that history, long suppressed and far more powerful for its silence.

My mother tells me the weather was perfect on the day my parents got Rick. It was late August or early September, she says. The air was cool, a pale autumnal blue, with just a few clouds scudding across the wide sky. Maybe she and my father had left their hotel to find some breakfast, or maybe they were out strolling just to take up the time before their meeting with the foster parents of the Ojibwe child they would adopt. In any case, my parents saw them: a man and a boy walking hand in hand. I imagine them, the man tall and thin, and the boy, his black hair shining under the September sun; their hands, the man's light-skinned and the boy's nut brown, clasped together tightly. As my parents watched, they turned together and entered a barber-shop. "Maybe that's him," my mother remembers thinking, and maybe she said as much to my father: "Maybe that's our boy." That night in the hotel, my father slept, his breath deep and slow. My mother sat in a chair holding the nut-brown boy, who cried, quiet wracking sobs, in her arms. In my imagination, my mother is entirely given over to love in this moment, overflow-ing with care for this miracle of black-haired boy, this new son.

This is an American captivity narrative. And like the captiv-ity narratives of the seventeenth, eighteenth, and nineteenth centuries, the emotional lives of the characters as well as the events that shape their perspectives are remarkably complex and convoluted. Like far too many of his generation and of the generations that preceded his, my brother was taken, stolen. Like other captors and their victims, my parents came to love their new young son and he them. One of the hard truths about *belonging* is that as much as the word speaks of love, of relation-ship, of loyalty, it also names possession, names ownership. To say that my brother belonged to my family or to me is to touch the marrow of racial history in the United States.

The word *captive* may be, in fact, inadequate, as is the word *belonging* understood as ownership. I want to shy away from these words, to talk around them without speaking or writing them at all. They do speak only a certain truth, not the whole truth. There was after all, from within the racial bunting, the deep, abiding love of mother for son, father for son, sisters for brother, and the urgency of need not only for food and shelter, but for the laying on of hands, for the holding, the wrestling, the kid sister's gentle pinch of an earlobe between thumb and forefinger on those nights when sleep was elusive. But there are some regimes of truth no amount of love, however transgres-sive, can surmount. Racial identity remained as an irreducible difference in the reception each of us received in the world.

That is, my parents, my sister, and I were perceived and treated as white, while my brother, despite the assimilationist policies that enabled his adoption by a white family, continued to be perceived and treated as a racial Other: the brown-skinned singularity bearing some degree of strangeness that could never be overcome, where overcoming was the *natural*, the of-course objective. He had been taken by the state and placed in the possession of a white family as part of a systematic effort to force assimilation and to put an end to Indian-ness altogether.

The Indian Adoption Project extended from 1958 to 1967. My brother's adoption took place in 1961. During this period the project placed 395 children of American Indian descent from sixteen states with white families (Herman, 2010). This number is deceiving, however. In 1969, a survey by the Association on American Indian Affairs reported that twenty-five to thirty percent of all Indian children in the United States had been taken from their birth families and tribes and placed in foster care, adoptive homes, orphanages, or boarding schools (Holt 2004, 4–5). The disparities between the numbers of white children and Indian children removed from families for such placements is stunning. Marilyn Holt notes that in South Dakota, for example, in 1960, "The Indian population was 3.6 percent of the total population, but 50 percent of all children in South Dakota foster care were Indian" (5). The placement of Indian children in orphanages and boarding schools had a much longer history than the practice of enforced transracial adoption, but all three practices share a common moral history. In fact, the practice of removing Indian children from their families, communities, and tribes, regardless of where those children were placed, was explained and justified by a system of morality coextensive with and supportive of prevailing racial ideologies.

In *Kill the Indian, Save the Man*, Churchill offers a powerful account of the degree to which, explicitly and by design, white policies that required and enforced the removal of American Indian children from their families and tribes for the purposes of (re)education through boarding schools (and we might reasonably extend his analyses to Indian orphanages and the state-sponsored transracial adoption of Indian babies) stipulated that this (re)education enforce the internalization of white ideology and, by extension, white morality. That is, explicitly and by design, Indian (re)education was a genocidal web of policy and practice intended to produce within those subject to it a sense of abhorrence for Indian-ness in themselves, in their birth families, and in their tribes. The transracial adoption of Indian children was designed to conscript Indian children into white racial projects by casting them in affiliative relationships with whites so their Indian identity might also be cast into doubt by their birth families and tribes. Regardless of the rhetoric of assimilation, adoptive Indian children would never become white; instead they would be a race-in-between visually marked as Other within the perceptive field of whiteness, and spiritually and culturally marked as Other within the perceptive field of Indian birth families and home communities. Additionally, this policy and practice, by design, confirmed and reinforced in the minds and spirits of whites conscripted in its service as adoptive families a sense of the *unbearable* rightness of being (white).

The practice of acknowledging whiteness as lived experience and of connecting that experience to histories of American racism can and really should be painful. We are the products, after all, of a history at least as terrible, as wicked, as it might be triumphant. The pain we feel in acknowledging our history is destructive only to the extent that we refuse to feel it or that we get stuck in it—that we forget that the reason for learning to remember is to learn also to change what we are and are capable of becoming. Whites cannot hope, I think, to join the band (to belong with and to the band) unless and until we recover from our individual and collective amnesia around our own racial histories. That is to say, if we who are raced white hope to heed Villanueva's call to recognize, honor, learn from the narratives of students and colleagues of color, and to participate in the creation of conditions in which such narratives may be offered, valued, and learned from, we will need to begin to learn and continue learning the practice of transmemoration: recalling and giving voice to individual and collective or historical memories of being raced white *without* displacing, disregarding, or over writing the remembrances of peoples of color. We will need to learn not only to accept, but to seek out the troubling of our memories, our narratives, the ways and degrees to which the collisions between narratives demand of us that we revise and resubmit in innumerable drafts that which we recall and believe we have learned through the practice of recollecting. We will need to begin and continue connecting our racial histories with the broader streams of racial history: with the ideologies and codifications of white supremacy in American social and political thought and law and the underwriting of predominantly white cultures by those ideologies.

Stories of raced-white experience unmoored from the social, and from their embeddedness in the long history of Western imperialism, exploitation, and domination, invite critique. Whatever the intentions of their authors, such stories collude with that history rather than intervene in it and sustain established racial orders by suppressing systematization and institutionalization of racism within them. The telling of raced-white stories in this way is as integral to the practices of implicit consent and self-veiling as these practices are to the perpetuation of racism and the reproduction of the social logics of white supremacy. As Sara Ahmed points out, the raced-white story told with the purpose of achieving absolution or transcendence affirms rather than disrupts the racialized quality of white social standing (2004, 4).

It is perhaps not surprising that narratives of raced-white experience tend in this direction, nor is it surprising that we do not know yet and must still learn ways of coming to know and of composing resisting stories. As Linda Alcoff writes,

> Social identities can confer motivations, or not, to develop a critical consciousness toward conventional beliefs and values. Such self-interested motivations can of course be overcome, as for example when the facts are too obvious to be ignored, but the point is that

in some groups a given justified claim will encounter more obstacles to its fair assessment than in other groups, depending on the social identity of the individuals involved. (2007, 44)

Alcoff goes on to argue that while oppressive societies resist recognition of the extent to which they are oppressive, there is, in fact, daily evidence of that oppression theoretically available to everyone. Our collective and individual failures to perceive the depth and breadth of racism, its systemic quality, constitute what Charles Mills refers to as a *consensual hallucination* (1999, 18). This cognitive dysfunction, writes Alcoff, is not a product of identity per se, but of historically produced "fits between knower and known" wherein ignorance is "an effect of inculcated practices common to a group" (2007, 49). The challenge, Alcoff suggests, for those of us who would take up a race-critical praxis is to discern, name, and critique the normative means by which we assess the nature of the everyday.

Before we can begin to engage in meaningful race-critical praxis in our communities or in our classrooms, we simply must engage critically with the racialized character of the epistemological practices of whiteliness. We need to acknowledge the degree to which both the objects of our study—whether that study takes place in school or out—and our modes of knowing are historical artifacts, not found objects per se, but formed through complex historical processes. We must denaturalize both our knowing and perceiving (Alcoff 2007, 51). We need, Alcoff argues, to recover our ability to resist, to actively withdraw consent to the reproduction of unjust and oppressive racial economies through the recovery of critical rationality (or critical ideation). For Alcoff, who draws heavily from the work of the Frankfurt School and of Horkheimer in particular, this labor is or will be constituted in part by "bring[ing] to consciousness the link between the social production of knowledge and the social production of society and thus [showing] that the production of knowledge is the product of conscious activity (even when it is not self-conscious about this fact)"—by recognizing, in other words, that "knowledge . . . reflects the current condition of human praxis" (54). But, Alcoff is quick to point out, because this work necessarily involves recognition that the objects or phenomena we describe are "the products of human praxis," the work of achieving the withdrawal of consent is or will be incomplete unless and until we have accounted not only for what is, but also what is possible. "We must acknowledge," she writes, "that we can, in effect, through a new praxis, choose the descriptions that we will make in the future" (54). The work Alcoff describes and advocates for is intellectual labor to be sure, but to the extent that this work engages future imagining, it is also labor deeply invested with hope. It is work that can easily be undermined by an overreliance on whiteliness: on either the established precepts or rules for knowledge production, traditionally conceived ("objectivity," "objective analysis," and the rehearsal of "fact") or impoverished understandings of the affective dimensions of knowledge-making and meaning-making processes.

It is fashionable, I think, in academe, to be dismissive of the affective dimensions of human experience and epistemologies, at least in part because of the degree to which the *agon* frames and shapes the discursive registers of our most acknowledged and legitimated knowledge-making practices. Alcoff suggests that this register disguises more than diminishes the affective dimensions of our knowing and coming to know. It is also true, however, that in other discourse communities (arguably, those very discourse communities that we are or say we are most invested in nurturing, sustaining, and transforming through antiracist activism and pedagogy), feeling, sensing, responsiveness to affective stimuli, the relational—and the narratives that braid affect with critical engagement in and through, with and against the materiality of lived experience—frame a different discursive register altogether. That we are dismissive of these ways of knowing and coming to know—snooty, even, about them—forecloses both the possibility of learning from them as well as learning to do them.

My own sense is that a deep-seated fear inflects the whiteliness embedded in and enacted through traditional conceptions of what might constitute "appropriate" or "legitimate" discursive registers for academic and for public or social argument. What if, we worry, in studying and discussing race and racism, we achieve not understanding but a moment of absolute and irreducible difference. What if we cannot persuade, cannot move one another, but find ourselves instead faced with what seem to be only two choices: to allow ourselves, our values and beliefs, the stories we have believed to be true about who we are and why and how we came to be so, to be shaken or shattered altogether; or to simply refuse to hear, to recognize, or to acknowledge one another's arguments at all. How, we worry, will we teach our way or learn our way out of the fact of fundamental impasse?

In September of 1985, the journal *Rhetoric Review* published an essay by Jim W. Corder entitled "Argument as Emergence: Rhetoric as Love." In this article, Corder, drawing on Doctorow, notes the ways and degrees to which all of us are always composing our lives, our experience, what we know and how we come to know, through narrative. "Each of us," Corder writes,

> forms conceptions of the world, its institutions, its public, private, wide, or local histories, and each of us is the narrative that shows our living in and through conceptions that are always being formed as the tales of our lives take their shape. . . . None of us lives without a history; each of us is a narrative. We're always standing some place in our lives, and there is always a tale of how we came to stand there, though few of us have marked carefully the dimensions of the place where we are or kept time with the tale of how we came to be there. (16)

As the essay unfolds, Corder calls readers to attend to those moments when narratives collide, resulting in what appear to be irreconcilable differences, and to

> the place where we are advocates of contending narratives (with their accompanying feelings and thoughts), where we are adversaries, each seeming to propose the repudiation or annihilation

of what the other lives, values, and is, where we are beyond being adversaries in that strange kind of argument we seldom attend to, where one offers the other a rightness so demanding, a beauty so stunning, a grace so fearful as to call the hearer to forego one identity for a startling new one. (1985, 24)

In these places and at these moments, Corder suggests, what we think of and value as reasoned argument fails to produce understanding, to enable change or transformation, though it may succeed as a slick display or performance in the context of the *agon.*

Instead of aiming for an end to the contest either through defeat or a dismissive turn away, in such places, at such moments in time, Corder says, we should learn to recognize argument not as finitude, but as emergence; we should learn, he argues, "to love before we disagree" (1985, 26). It is through this recognition and this learning that hope is reasonable and change or learning made realizable. "The arguer," Corder writes,

> must at once hold his or her identity and give it to the other, learning to live—and argue—provisionally. . . .We must keep learning as speakers/narrators/arguers (and as hearers). We can learn to dispense with what we imagined was absolute truth and to pursue the reality of things only partially knowable. We can learn to keep adding pieces of knowledge here, to keep rearranging pieces over yonder, to keep standing back and turning to see how things look elsewhere. We can learn that our narrative/argument doesn't exist except as it is composed and that the "act of composing can never end," as Doctorow has said. (28–29)

This, Corder argues, is the substance of invention, the invocation of "a commodious language" capable of pressing back against closure, against the world's expressed desires for speed, efficiency, and certainty in service of the creation of time for plenitude and for care.

In a similar vein, though through a different discipline, moral theologian James Carse writes of the distinction between finite and infinite games. Finite games, like *agon*, are played in order to eliminate one's opponents: to win. Infinite games, Carse suggests, are played in ways that insure the continuation of the game—in order that more and more players may join. Both Corder and Carse recognize that infinite play may require that the player or actor, the arguer or learner, may at times be required to get lost in composing, to go on alone or at least without certainty that one is not alone; but always, for both writers, the reason to go on is the search for, the hope of, company. Both Corder and Carse advocate for a willingness to get lost as a way of moving, and for learning as the continual emergence of readiness for surprise, for the accident that shakes one to the core, that shifts one's direction and vantage point. And this is a conception of argument quite distinct from a conception of argument as the construction of an immutable narrative plotline, of claims and supporting logics that are indisputable or immune to challenge. This is, as Corder writes, a conception of argument as love, the long lean into the Other in search of the points of articulation—the joints—between narratives. Here, argument is love in search of the point of opening between self and other. This is the exercise of creative ideation: the ability to form thoughts about worlds not yet seen by building upon, but not being limited by, history and lived experience. Creative ideation engages the imagination in conceiving of and working toward enabling conditions for a range of future alterities. And creative ideation is relational at root. It is the intellectual labor of future perfect: building on deep engagement with the question *who are you?* and, given this, rising toward—embracing even—with unfettered intimacy the question *what will we have done?*

In October of 2007, a very large RV decorated with a giant logo advertising the Hello Love Experiment pulled up and parked in front of our house in suburban Lincoln. Its occupants, an HBO film crew, piled out onto the sidewalk and unloaded their equipment. They had come to film an interview with me as part of a documentary about the role of love in social transformation. The documentary project has, I believe, fallen on hard times, and I'm not sure it will ever be completed, but the experiment lives on. In short, the Hello Love story is that a group of friends in Los Angeles began experimenting with living their conviction that we are all love by standing on street corners holding signs and greeting passersby with a smile and the words "Hello Love" (http://helloloveexperiment.org/). Pursuing their experiment, they garnered funding for a Hello Love tour, both for the purposes of promoting their practice of love as a socially transformative force and filming their experiences for a documentary on love as they went along. Maybe you've seen the YouTube video chronicling a similar experiment, the Free Hugs Campaign. If you haven't you should check it out.[3] The Hello Love experiment is offered in a similar spirit. I confess that when I watch these things, my heart and my mind go to war with each other. On one hand, I'm terribly moved, and on the other I'm so cynical, and embarrassed even, that I'm capable of being moved by what seems to me to be somehow so overwhelmingly sweet and utterly naïve (whiteliness frosted in sugar).

In any case, the Hello Love RV rolled up to my house and within a matter of minutes my dining room was transformed into a film set. I was being interviewed about love in the work of antiracism. Now I admit I'm as conflicted about articulating my sense of the role of love within the antiracism movement as I am about my responses to social experiments like Free Hugs and Hello Love. One wants to say, "Well, of course. Love must be self-evidently good, necessary even, to labors for social justice and for the eradication of racism, in particular. And yet, as necessary as love may be, it is not, I think, sufficient." I said this in my interview and the words visibly stung my interviewers (all of whom were white) so that I wished I hadn't felt the necessity to speak the thought aloud. I admired their experiment; I really did. And I was touched by what seemed to me at the time to be

---

3. Free Hugs Campaign—Official Page. (n.d.), video clip, YouTube, uploaded September 26, 2006, http://www.youtube.com/watch?v=vr3x_RRJdd4.

some lovely thread of innocence in their faith. The insufficiency of love (traditionally and ideally conceived), though, must be named and has less to do with any quality inherent to the feeling itself than with the ways in which the strategic deployment of simulations of an emotion like love can too easily work to efface the historical conditions that produce oppressions like racism and the lived reality of racism—that no amount of love, in and of itself, can ameliorate or eradicate. And the fact of feeling what one thinks is love can also make one feel morally superior, somehow. As if you've done enough just by feeling that loving feeling that those on the receiving end ought to reciprocate or at least feel grateful. Or ought to acknowledge that however anyone else may be, you, at least, are a loving person, a good person.

The danger of love in the antiracism movement (and in activist pedagogies as well) is that in our conviction that to *feel* this way is *good*, makes us *good* people, we may hide our own complicity with racism from ourselves. While we can and should recognize that racial categories and attending racial identities are socially constructed, the maintenance of any form of social order depends upon the consent of those governed by that order, regardless of whether they/we are well served by it, benefit from it, or are disenfranchised or oppressed by it. Consent can be manufactured, but agency is active even within the production of consensus. To join productively in antiracism work requires our recognition of the extent to which all of us do, in fact, consent to participate in the maintenance of things-as-they-are. That is to say, as Ellen Messr-Davidow has written in other contexts, "There are no innocent bystanders; if you're standing by, you aren't innocent" (2002, 288). We may know that racism is evil and those who wittingly or unwittingly participate in it are wrong, but it does not logically follow that those of us who know this are, by virtue of our knowledge, free of racism. The hard reality is that love, alone, will not save us.

Creative ideation is no more sufficient in and of itself than are pursuant or critical ideation taken either singly or together as a pair. But to recognize and act upon the recognition of the mutual contingency, the interdependence of all three ways of learning and of knowledge production in the context of composing an emergent race-critical consciousness, is to begin at least to create and sustain the conditions in which antiracist praxis is conceivable and practicable. To attempt to narrate, to think, to feel, and to compose one's experience of these three modes of ideation in an all-at-once way (to channel, for a moment, Buckminster Fuller), does not prevent or even agitate against the possibility of failure. What the attempt does do, I think, is to sustain the possibility of ongoing learning even and especially in the face of failure—when it may well be that we learn most deeply and lastingly. Far from being facile—an easily mastered mindscape—the all-at-onceness of pursuant, critical, and creative ideation is as wobbly as a three-legged stool on a moving ship. The divinity and infinity, the plenitude of learning available to us in the exercise of attempting to find and sustain balance, is not in our mastery of the thing, but rather in our willingness to stay with the labor even in the face of its apparent impossibility, to stay with one another even as we are broken, fail, and fall.

Both of my parents were professors at a small university in rural western Pennsylvania. My father taught piano, composition, and music history and my mother taught Jeffersonian and African American history. Some of my earliest memories are of waiting in one or the other of their offices for my parents to finish their work for the day. When I was in kindergarten, my dad would pick me up after school and take me to his office while he completed his last lessons. I would crawl under one of the two baby grand pianos in his office and let the music his students pounded out shake my very bones. When I was older, I walked from my elementary school to my mother's office, stopping on the way at Phero's Market to buy a Hostess cherry pie to eat while I waited for her. After I had finished my homework and the department secretary had gone home for the day, I was allowed to sit at the main office desk and pretend I was the secretary (my most cherished ambition at the time). The history department offices were located within a suite and separated from one another and from the main office by glass cubicle dividers. Because those dividers didn't reach the ceiling, if the office inhabitants raised their voices (which seemed to me to happen quite frequently), you could hear every word from the secretary's desk. So it was that from a very early age, I became quite knowledgeable about university politics, about academic infighting, and about the kind and degree of misery academic conflicts can engender in combatants.

One day, as I sat at the secretary's desk cracking Doublemint gum (a practice I associated with being a secretary) and pretending to type memos, I overheard my mother arguing with a university administrator, an African American woman, in the department's conference room. Their voices, which had been low and measured for what seemed like quite a while, began to rise in pitch and volume. As the conversation continued and I listened, I knew that my mother had started to cry. During the late sixties and early seventies, my mom designed and began to offer a course called Black Experience in American Film. As the first and one of the only courses offered in African American studies by the university, the course was immensely popular with black students and regularly over enrolled with well over fifty registrations (a remarkable feat for a school with a rather limited population of students of color and only a few thousand students overall). Occasionally, my brother and I were allowed to go with my mother when she taught that class to watch the movies she was showing and to listen in on the discussions that followed. We would sit beside students we knew through my parents and pretend that we, too, were in college and qualified to be there.

In any case, by the midseventies, some controversy had erupted around the teaching of that course. The question my mother and the administrator seemed to be debating was whether she, as a white woman, was qualified to teach Black Experience in Film, no matter the quality of her book learning.

How could she, a white woman, speak to the matter of black experience, the administrator wanted to know. How could my mother avoid reproducing the very stereotypes she sought to expose in the films she studied by virtue of the fact that she did not, could not, in fact, share the individual and collective experiences of her black students? My mother told me recently that she understood the administrator to be arguing that the films ought to be buried and forgotten, for the damage their representations of blacks inflicted was too devastating to be mitigated by analysis, even of their racism. Who was my mother, the black administrator wanted to know, to be teaching such a course?

My mother fought back, I remember, though I don't recall what exactly she said in her own defense. Ultimately, however, my mom gave up. She had tried, she told the administrator, to provide a course for the university's black students that would recognize and address the ways in which their experiences and shared history might have been shaped by race and racism. She thought she'd done a good thing for them and done it well. But if the administration couldn't understand why the course was important and refused to provide the institutional support needed to offer the course, then she would withdraw it from the department's offerings and never teach it again. My mom told me recently that students later complained about the course being withdrawn from the department's offerings, but even so she felt she couldn't teach it and chose not to fight for it as she perceived the battle to be already lost.

My mom was a courageous activist during those years and her courage remains undepleted now as she struggles with the effects of multiple sclerosis and the vicissitudes of aging with a chronic illness. But even back then I knew something died in my mom that day. I know she continued to mentor individual students of color, but she no longer participated in the same ways she had done for many years in larger struggles for racial justice on campus or in the community. She withdrew from what I would now understand to be everyday antiracism as she did from the public work of antiracism. My mom was,

I still believe, embittered by that argument; she felt attacked, misunderstood, misrepresented, and unappreciated. And for a long time her response to the event was anger, defensiveness, and defiance.

There are several strands in this story that are worth noticing. The first is that, whether one agrees with the arguments of the administrator or not, her focus on the impacts, the effects of racism, is significant. Peoples of color and their white allies within the antiracism movement are and need to be concerned with the lived experiences of peoples of color under conditions of racism, with the materiality of racism in the lives of peoples of color. The problems that drive the antiracism movement are, in the first instance, concrete: what quality of education and healthcare are available to people of color? How can limitations to equal access and disparities in quality be meaningfully addressed? What are the employment opportunities for peoples of color and how can we ensure that peoples of color have equal opportunity for gainful employment and are fairly and equally compensated for their labor? And so on. In the case of the university administrator, the question at stake seemed to orient around the impacts on students of color of watching, in the context of a college classroom, films that represent blacks in demeaning, disrespectful, racist ways. Could this ever be a learningful experience for students of color; or was the experience more likely to do harm? The administrator was unconcerned with my mother's intentions, as unmoved by my mother's expertise as a historian and track record as a local civil rights activist as she was unconcerned about whether or not my mother liked her, whether they had ever been or would continue to be friends. Her only concern was whether there was anything worthwhile to be learned by black students from studying the history of American racism in film that would outweigh the potential harm caused by being exposed (again) to that racism in the context of a college classroom.

A second and related critical strand is my mother's virtual abandonment of public antiracism following this challenge to her authority by a woman of color. Unable to convince the administrator of the intellectual and disciplinary value of her course and her pedagogy, and unable to navigate the discrepancies between her sense of herself as a good person, a well-intentioned and even righteous advocate for students of color, and her sense of how she was perceived by the administrator, my mom, for all intents and purposes, gave up a labor to which she had previously dedicated tremendous time, energy, and passion. She abandoned, in some sense, the hope that she might join productively and meaningfully with her students and colleagues of color in ongoing collective struggles for increasing racial justice.

The collision of interests (impacts versus intentions) evinced in the argument between my mother and the administrator is not unique to their encounter, but common, I think, as peoples of color and whites come together to combat racism. Nor are the administrator's and my mother's failures to speak, to listen, to recognize, and to acknowledge one another unique to their particular encounter with one another. Finally, and sadly, my mother's stormy departure from the field is not an isolated retreat, but part of a pattern of collective retreat by whites and peoples of color from the possibility of actualizing multiracial, antiracist solidarity and coalition. My mother talks now about the importance of learning to stay in service of solidarity and ongoing coalition: learning to speak, learning to write, learning to learn with and for one another—even in the face of what seem to be catastrophic failures of understanding, communication, performativity. And it is this talk of revision, and the thinking informing this talk, that constitutes the legacy she passes forward.

Both my mother and I have had to learn what it might mean to stay, what staying might require of us, and how to stay well. We are still learning, and perhaps more than this we are unlearning. Whiteliness has framed for far too long the stories each of us tells about our family, our work, our lives. Whiteliness inflects our overreliance on credentials, whether we claim our expertise based on life experience, on the kind and quality of our relationships, or on our degrees. Whiteliness is our fallback position—the wall our backs are up against—when conversations get hard. Whiteliness conditions our defensive sense that what truly matters is our essential goodness, our good intentions, or our innocence. Whiteliness drives us away from the company we most need when our own complicity with racism is at stake. Whiteliness presses our thinking into service for its preservation and reproduction, forks our tongues as we speak, or drives us into stony silence when the stories of ourselves we live and tell provoke not approbation and gratitude, but critical challenge and resistance.

Who are you? Who are you to do this work? These questions might, if we open ourselves to them, unsettle us, disturbing our sense of complacency about our ways of being and doing in the world. But the point is not merely to be disturbed; the work of antiracism is undergirded by critical thinking about thinking itself—about the range of implicit investments in knowing, coming to know, and the making of meaning that frame the narratives we construct, tell, and perform in our everyday lives. To be productively disturbed requires, I think, that we begin to examine the thinking that leads us to craft of our experience points of rhetorical innocence or transcendence from which to speak and act nonperformatively against racism; that is to say, with good intentions, but to little or no productive effect. To be usefully disturbed requires that we begin to connect both our experience and thought to collective memory and to history, and not just the inherited memories of ancestors and histories of people we claim as our own, but to the memories and histories of others. We need to remember without dismissing the memories of others and to historicize without suppressing the interrelations among and between all of our histories. Finally, to be usefully disturbed requires us to acknowledge critically the extent to which the ways we have learned to think white and whitely, by design, elicit our consent to things-as-they-are. We need to unlearn the thinking that forecloses on the possibility of tomorrow being different from today. And that means we need to unlearn the thinking that manufactures our consent to racism by occluding the fact of our agency.

Pursuant, critical, and creative ideation are foundational to antiracist epistemology and rhetoric. Each requires mindful turning and *re*-turning inward and outward, from one's own story of racialization and emerging race consciousness to the stories of others and back again. No one I know enacts any or all of these ideations fully and yet, taken together, even as antiracist activists and educators struggle for balance in a broken and shifting world, these are means by which the endless turnings and re-turnings antiracism demands of us all are transformed from insanity to reengagement. Epistemologically speaking, these are the means by which we might catch a glimpse that surprises us, however brief, of a threshold, an opening, a way to move toward and for one another in felicitous pursuit and composition of our collective hope.

3

WRESTLING WITH ANGELS

The last time I tried to save my brother I drove from Minnesota to Wisconsin on a gray February day. The snow lay in dirty piles along the roadside and my car plowed dutifully through the slush that covered the tarmac. I was feeling good. This time I had a plan. I had been dispatched by my family innumerable times to extract my brother from trouble, but always before these journeys had been adrenaline-filled flights borne of crisis, with little or no planning preceding them.

When we were still young and innocent, I was sent to convince my brother that we really did have to remove the plastic swimming pool filled with water and tadpole eggs from his second floor bedroom even though the notion of growing our own frogs was exceptionally tantalizing. At fourteen, less innocent, I learned to drive when asked to please take home my brother, who had drunk far too much at a party hosted by one of my parents' colleagues. With just enough sense left to fold himself into the backseat of his Capri and instruct me in the fine art of pushing in the clutch to shift gears before passing into a deep and boozy sleep, my brother never heard the grinding of gears nor felt the lurch of the car as I drove the ten miles home, praying for an absence of cops. Much later, with still less innocence, I drove like a bat out of hell to New Jersey to gather up my brother after he lay down on the rails that carried commuters from the suburbs into New York City, but was picked up by the transit police before being crushed; flew from one coast to the other to extract him from a crack house and bring him home for one more round of treatment; telephoned every hospital in Oregon until I found him drying himself out in a psych ward.

For a long time, I envied my brother. I imagined him immersing himself in oblivion, secure in the knowledge that I would come before he reached too far toward emptiness. I even tried the immersion once or twice myself, testing the possibility that I too would be saved. I was, but never wholly. And I learned that there are some things from which one cannot be saved; resignation to the misery and squalor of those wicked places in the soul is far worse, I learned, than expending the energy required to wrestle with the angels. I also learned that there are times when defeating an angel simply isn't possible; one's only hope lies in outlasting the struggle.

As I drove through that ugly February day, I felt contained and centered. This time, I thought, I wouldn't even try to extract Rick. I came instead with an offer of assistance, a support structure, I told myself, by which he might extract himself and his family from poverty, from the interferences of the state, from what I saw as the misery and squalor of their lives. And love. I came with the unconditional love of a sister and the intensity, the certainty, of that love carried me over the miles.

The car jounced up the long driveway, through the ruts of snow, past increasingly run-down homes, until I came to my brother's double-wide and the rusting hulks of scrap cars languishing beneath the drifts. He came to the door smiling at the surprise of my arrival, but the smile didn't reach his eyes, which were cool and wary. I asked him to walk with me. Having slid into a coat, he came out into the driveway and we talked together. I laid it out—the plan in all its exquisite perfection, down to the last detail. I couldn't tell if he was listening. Always the master of non sequitur, he told me that he never wanted to make anyone feel the fear he had experienced the night he encountered aliens while walking alone through the woods. I couldn't tell if he was joking. He demurred. We went inside, into the heat and filth. His wife and children gathered in the living room to listen as I pressed him to accept the plan. He turned his back on me. And when he turned once more to face me, I watched as, for a moment, all emotion in a receding tide seemed to wash away from him. And then rage crashed across his face like a tsunami. His wife and children scattered like flotsam and jetsam before the tide. He picked up a chair and hurled it at me. "Why won't all you FUCKING WHITE PEOPLE just leave me alone!" he screamed. Then he stormed out the door and into the awful grayness of the afternoon.

The truths that compose our lives, that bind us one to another, are made not of bone, but of thin and fragile membrane. They rip in these moments, shredding all conviction, tearing us loose even from those relations we believed were most certain, and most knowable. Love, alone, is never enough, and love that disguises the exercise of whiteliness is no love at all.

I drove home alone and the silence was absolute. The turning of wheels through slush, the rush of wind over the hood and windshield, seemed to produce no sound at all. Our mutual betrayals of our secret histories had been spectacular. Each of us had dared to speak a certain truth, to expose and with our words slice clean through a strand of that thin, fragile membrane that held us one to another.

Rick's words, spoken like Moses, with all the weight of a terrible history, split us both into past and present: ourselves and yet, also, our peoples; ourselves and yet, also, our filial relations; brother and sister, childhood companions and friends and yet, also, a man and a woman whose memories, experiences, ways of knowing, and knowledge seemed to have been sliced clean through by the fact of racism come before, even now, and still to come. Histories of oppression as the object of study may feel generalized and abstract. But in the lives of those who are subjects of and subject to those histories, the past is never neatly contained within the pages of books or even within stories crafted of collective memory. These histories are lived. And there are moments, like this one shared between my brother and me, when, in just a few seconds, an ember of lived history bursts suddenly into flaming catastrophe, exploding the here and now and tearing one's universe apart.

Perhaps it goes without saying that addiction and mental illness, both of which I believe my brother suffers from, are complex phenomena. My sister reminds me that not everything in our lives, in my brother's life, can be distilled down to his experience of racism. This is true. But that experience, largely unnamed and unacknowledged in our lives together, certainly played a role in our individual and collective dysfunctions. As a friend of mine is fond of saying, racism is crazy-making. And like addiction and mental illness, racism exposes not only the ways in which it makes those subject to racism crazy, but also the ways in which its perpetrators, consciously or no, intentionally or no, are also made crazy, not in exactly the same ways but critically, by the relations we create and sustain through racism's exercise. My brother might have been a little bit nuts, but the truth was that I was crazy too.

Addiction and mental illness do not—and this is part of their tragedy—banish all ability to know and speak the truth. Even from the chaotic mess of consciousness such diseases produce in the mind and soul, catastrophic, blinding, anguishing insights may be formed and spoken. Rick had spoken just such a truth. Similarly, the crazy-making qualities of white supremacist ideology and of whiteliness do not destroy our ability to speak certain truths; rather, they subvert the integrity of those truths, bending and warping our powers of discernment until we cling to what we believe we know as if there is nothing else to be known, nothing else worth knowing. I hadn't been completely wrong, but I had been a lot wrong—enough to do harm.

The long slow burn of history as lived experience carried different and unequal weight and produced different and unequal effects in the lives of my brother and me. As connected as I felt and still feel to my brother, as much love as I felt and feel, as painful as our estrangement was and continues to be, the history that shaped so much of his life shaped only a thin slice

of mine. Our experiences of racism were so different in quality and degree that, in the aftermath of our battle, I could not
pretend to either analogous or empathic understanding. I had
come to my brother deluded by the exceptionally whitely and
self-centered notion that I could see his life and its complexities
more clearly than he could himself—that I could offer a plan,
which, if he only followed it, would rather quickly and easily
repair him and his world. And in so doing, I had obscured from
myself, at least, the extent to which the logics of white supremacy seeped into and out of my perspectives of the world and my
interpretation of the matter that I found there. Finally, I realized that there are choices one makes, actions one takes that
cannot be undone, compensated for, repaired, or apologized
for adequately. What transforms a rather innocuous choice into
a terrible one is not one's intent to cause harm, but the actualization of harm, the effects of one's choices on the lives of others. Guilt does not transform relations ruptured by such choices
and neither, ultimately, does love, traditionally or whitely conceived and practiced.

Unwittingly, my brother and I had found our way to that
collision of narratives described by Corder. Softly and insinuat-
ingly, I spun my story to Rick, offered it to him as if it were a
gift, without having considered too much or too well the hidden costs for him of accepting it. Rick didn't so much offer his
story to me as slam me with it, repudiating not only the gift,
but also the tissue of lies that had marred our relations from
their inception. He annihilated the deathly silence that had
surrounded the power, the heft, of racism in our lives. It was
Rick, finally and perhaps paradoxically, who in and for that
moment brought us, brought me, to the terrible and beautiful,
anguishing place beyond the adversarial, to what Corder calls
"that strange kind of argument we seldom attend to, where
one offers the other a rightness so demanding, a beauty so
stunning, a grace so fearful as to call the hearer to forego one
identity for a startling new one" (1985, 24). The challenge, I
knew, as I drove the long miles home, was now as it had been

for as long as I had been committed to the work of antiracism, to decenter in order that I might again and more fully this time listen, attend, and learn.

I had stood before my brother in that terrible moment not merely as Frankie, but also as the instantiation of white womanhood—the figure of the angel who offers salvation, but delivers hell. To discern myself in that figure, I had to attempt, at least, to re-member what I had done; I needed to perceive and make sense somehow of a performance that had not been mine alone, not merely a product of my individual choices and actions, but also an effect of the social and historical force of racialization and of racism. But there was even more than this to do. For snaking through that sense of self as self-alone is the conviction that we are only responsible for our selves and not for our subjectivities. To create conditions in which learning might be possible, I had to at least inquire into the depth and degree of my connectedness to those social and historical forces that I both embodied and enacted on that day. In the context of a whitely world, I had acted "reasonably." To learn and thus to change the conditions of possibility for being differently and resistingly in that world, I needed to become unhinged as it were from that reasonability. I needed to study my socially perceived self not as a familiar and an intimate, but as a stranger. I needed to lean into that socially perceived self to see how much of the self I experience myself or believe myself to be might be reflected there. This is the epistemological and rhetorical practice of decentering.

The sculptor Elizabeth King, who experiments with perspective in her work, plays with the word and concept of *pupil*: the pupil that is the aperture of the eye, the pupil who studies, but also the *pupilla*—the miniature version of the self that can be seen by leaning in to see one's own reflection in the eye of an Other (1999, 12). Decentering is like this. I try to shift the focus of the aperture of my mind's eye, to open it wider, to let in more light. I need to see, to know differently. I try to move myself so that what I can see of the world changes. I need to see, to know the world differently. I lean into memory as if into my brother's eyes to see myself as I am reflected there. I need to see, to know myself differently. Slowly and imperfectly, I am making strange for myself what had been familiar of myself and myself-in-relation. Haltingly, but stubbornly, even as I labor to shift the quality of my gaze and to make a study of myself and the world, I am also making myself available to and aware of the gaze of the stranger. I need to be moved by that gaze, to be changed by it. I need to yield my self to it. To decenter is to come to consciousness that I am seen, at least on occasions such as these, not merely as self qua self, but also as self qua whitely. And more. To decenter is to see for myself my self qua whitely.

I can't. The work is impossible. I try anyway. I fail, but I see differently than I saw and am not what I was when I began. I try again.

Decentering as a way of re-searching, and thus of producing new knowledge about the self-in-the-world, is akin to that literacy Min-Zhan Lu terms "critical affirmation." For Lu, critical affirmation recognizes and acknowledges the "yearning for individual agency shared by individuals across social divisions without losing sight of the different material circumstances which shape this shared yearning and the different circumstances against which each of us must struggle when enacting such a yearning" (1999, 173). A fundamental condition of possibility for a practice like decentering is a desire morphing toward veritable need to act in and on the world "to end oppression rather than to empower a particular form of self, group or culture" (173). Critical affirmation resonates with the work of antiracism particularly in the care, the attention, and the intentionality with which its practitioners attend to the material conditions that shape differential experience across racial (and other identity) lines. Like critical affirmation, decentering is aimed at destabilizing forms of self-ideation that nonreflexiveness about "the paradox of privilege" engender: that "the very system of oppression one deplores and has interests in fighting against often confers certain privileges upon oneself" (176). And like critical affirmation, decentering treats experience—in particular the experience of collision between the self as experienced and the self as socially perceived—as "a possible site for critical intervention on the formation of one's self and the material conditions of one's life" (174).

The necessity for a practice like decentering makes itself felt in the dynamism of human relations and, especially, in the reach toward an Other and a rebuff. Antiracism is oppositional in both theory and practice. In some sense, decentering is the practice of taking that rebuff seriously. Rather than deflecting or stomping away, abandoning both the work of antiracism and the alliances that make doing the work both possible and meaningful, decentering enables staying and shouldering the burden of doing the work the rebuff calls us to do.

To decenter requires that we go to the space in-between self and other, but also to the space in-between one's idea of one's self and that which one is perceived as being: "Our socially perceived self within the systems of perception and classification and the networks of community in which we live" (Alcoff 2005, 92–93). Shaped by racial ideology, these perceptive and classificatory systems and networks limit the conditions of possibility for all of us, albeit unequally. Further, as Linda Alcoff points out, our lived experience often rubs up against our public identity; we don't understand, don't experience ourselves as being only that which our public identity names us as being. Our lived experience exceeds and overflows that public face (93). Thus we can and often do claim that we are not what we are perceived as being.

This claim has long-standing importance in the resistance to racial oppression: it is one means by which peoples of color have spoken back to racial stereotypes and to the social, political, and economic restrictions and exclusions that sustain the racial state. But this claim has also played and continues to play a critical role in white denial not only of the demands for racial equality by peoples of color, but also of the existence and continuing impact of racism itself. The claim is one integral way in which whites have shut out and shut down dialogues about race and racism when the collision of narratives seems imminent or has already occurred.

One of the hard realities, I think, is that racism, as a historical reality and a material force in the shaping of social identities, constructs differing, counterposed subject positions and subjectivities in and for whites and peoples of color. Ideologies of race, racism, and white supremacy, in other words, work differently and with different effects, different weights, on peoples of color than on whites. Put most simply, such ideologies work within white consciousness to confirm and enforce the internalization of white supremacy while simultaneously working on the consciousnesses of peoples of color to confirm and enforce the internalization of racial oppression. For peoples of color within the antiracism movement, very often the struggle with regard to decentering is to become conscious of and to wrestle against the internalization and reexternalization of the very kind of whitely voices that assault oneself and one's peoples on a daily basis—to resist and unlearn the reenactment of one's own oppression as an internal process. For both peoples of color and for whites, decentering involves bringing to light, to consciousness, those learned and now habitual ways of thinking, feeling, sensing ourselves in relation to ourselves, and ourselves in relation to others, that shape our everyday lives, that shape how we live in the world, what we do, our beingness in a quotidian sense.

When we create narratives about ourselves as well as when we receive Other narratives, we speak, write, and make meaning from our social locations; the narratives we create and the sense we make of the relations between our stories and those of others are both enabled and constrained by the interpretive horizons those social locations shape and frame. Each interpretive horizon is constituted by "the range of vision that includes everything that can be seen from a particular vantage point" (Gadamer quoted in Alcoff 2005, 95). That horizon, however, is not only the means by which we perceive, but also the condition in which we perceive. That is, our interpretive horizons possess both content and location (95). Ideologies of race, racism, and white supremacy form a critical and significant slice of each of our interpretive horizons. These are lenses through which we have all been taught to see, to feel, to know the world. To suggest that our horizons are closed, however, or immutable is merely an abstraction. "The horizon," Alcoff writes, "is a substantive perspectival location from which the interpreter looks out at the world, a perspective that is always present but that is open and dynamic, with a temporal as well as physical dimension, moving into the future and into new spaces as the subject moves" (95). We do, in fact, change, for we do, in fact, learn. In fact, I would argue, the desire and the will to learn is hardwired into all of us and is part of what our racialization works to suppress in us when we are called or pressed into service as participants in multiracial dialogues about race and racism.

The idea of participating in conversations about race and racism, let alone leading or attempting to sponsor and facilitate a discussion about race and racism whether informally (as with a group of friends) or formally (in a community meeting, a classroom, or a writing center), provokes anxiety and fear in many of us. For some, these feelings emerge from a conviction that no good can come of such exchanges—that increased discord or disappointment are inevitable outcomes. Others believe that such dialogues produce depths of rage and shame that cannot be productively addressed either in conversation between friends or in more formal educational settings.

Recently, in public policy debates around the wisdom and value of teaching Chicana(o) and African American studies, in particular, figures such as Arizona Superintendent of Public Instruction, Tom Horne, have claimed that the purpose of such programs, in which dialogue about race and racism is immanent, can only be subversion—to foment a revolutionary movement among people of color and to cultivate a sense of national shame among whites. Framed in this way, dialogues about race and racism constitute traitorous attempts to undermine white pride, and white national and communal unity.

These discussions give voice to histories that Horne and others call into question less for their historical accuracy than for the perceived consequences of giving voice to them; they are, in Horne's words, "a downer" (Ethnic Studies 2011). For Horne, and for many of us, though associating ourselves with Horne may feel abhorrent to us, the choice such collisions seem to present falls between denial, oblivion, or pain and what feel like the faintest of possibilities for understanding. In these moments in which we encounter Other histories, Other accounts of lived experience—stories that disrupt narratives we have most carefully constructed to support our sense of ourselves in the world and the sense we would have the world make of us—too often we choose not to go beyond the moment of apparently irreducible difference; we choose, instead, to treat these collisions as endings, abrupt and final.

The real work of white supremacy can be read here: in the closure of material opportunity in the classroom, in the professions, in social life in all its forms, and in the body politic, to peoples of color who cannot change the color of their skin and who would not even if they could; who, recognizing the cost, will not excise the histories of alliance and survivance, the cultures of vitality and strength that shape their sense of self regardless of how those histories and cultures are inscribed in whitely imagination. The promise white supremacy holds out to peoples of color is always a lie: that whiteness plays no role in determinations of the worth and potential of individuals in any context, nor in the range of material opportunities that might be made available to individuals or groups; that responsibility for the limits or finitudes of material opportunity resides with peoples of color, themselves.

We can read, if we will, the closure of opportunity that white supremacy enacts in the classrooms and the writing centers where we teach writing and rhetoric, even in those courses and centers we design with the express intention of making ourselves and our students ready for informed and adept citizenship in what we hope may become a robust multiracial democracy.

Victor Villanueva has urged the field of writing and rhetoric studies to note the ways in which our "blindness" to race and racism compromises our ability to theorize our work more fully, to practice our work more responsibly, and to contribute meaningfully to the democratization of our institutions (2006). Vershawn Ashanti Young has called the discipline to attend to the disjunctions between our claims to support and enact principles that might attend education for a more fully realized democracy, particularly the principles outlined in the 1974 NCTE Resolution on Students' Right to Their Own Language, and the practice of advocating code switching. Young notes the failure of democracy-in-action implicit in communicating to students of color that the language of power is fixed and immoveable, that their home languages are all very well and good where they come from but not in the college classroom, that there are no ways of knowing and no knowledge produced within their home language communities that have value in academia or in the professional world. Echoing and amplifying the work of Elspeth Stuckey on the violence of literacy, Young takes note of the lie we perpetuate when we claim that if only students will learn to think, read, and speak in whitely English when they move in academic or professional communities, they will not be subject to the force of racism—as if racism is an effect of peoples of color not talking and writing right (whitely) (2010).

Our relationships to our languages are always predicated on the affiliative relation. As Elaine Richardson writes in her essay "'To Protect and Serve': African American Female Literacies," "Mothers transmit their language into their children who develop facility with it. In this sense we all inherit the condition/ing of our mother if she has a word in our socialization. But, more basically, our language, our mother tongue, is at least partly how we know what we know" (2002, 677). Later, in her book *African American Literacies*, Richardson narrates her own experience as a student writer of color in the writing center as demeaning. This experience, she suggests, confirmed her sense as an undergraduate that in order to succeed academically she would have to excise aspects of herself that were rooted in her identity as a black woman (2003, 1–2). Not only are demands for such excisions unfair, oppressive even, they are impossible demands to meet. Not because of the determinacy of our raced conditions, but because no one can unthink history or dis-member the conditions of one's own coming to being. Even if we would choose such a path, forgetting is always partial and provisional. The trace remains.

For me, and I suspect for many progressive whites, the idea that we might share any of Horne's ideology, his worldviews, is deeply distressing. And yet the practice of decentering might take us exactly there: to those buried, secret, interior places where what we feel and think coincides with that which we know to be wrong, small, and mean. Decentering as activists, as teachers, or as scholars might also demand of us that we begin to see the ways in which the values, traditions, and epistemologies of our families, our communities, and our professions similarly coincide with, sustain, and reproduce the substance as well as the perspectival location of someone like Tom Horne. And when we begin to perceive in this way, we cannot despise Tom Horne the man without also despising ourselves in what is really a pointless exercise in loathing.

Keith Gilyard writes that although "it is entirely possible that racist verbal constructs are directly responsible for racist actions . . . it is also possible for one to act humanely even while operating inside a certain language of inhumanity" (1999, 51). To engage in activism, teaching, and/or scholarship that touches on the transformative, white antiracists don't need either the vitriol or the self-aggrandizement that emerges from moral binaries that fall along the lines of "he is evil; I am not," but a deep enough recognition of our need and desire to be and become at the border or joint, such that we can begin to discern the both-and. We need to notice the degree to which, within our socially perceived identities, our lived experiences, and our embodiment of those identities within our roles as activists, teachers, and scholars, we may be enacting that which we abhor even as we are imagining ourselves as ones who resist. If white antiracism is to be performative, it must entail recognizing the limits of whitely discourse. As Gilyard writes, "What one cannot do . . . when locked inside the discourse of 'race' is to show the way out of that position. Thus, one is implicated to the degree that that discourse is delimiting. The 'degree' is what we need to investigate further and continue to do so deeply and frequently" (51). Decentering might be understood in this context as the practice of inquiry—as a sustained, purposeful, critical investigation of the degree to which we, whitely teachers and scholars, are in fact implicated. Our collective and individual focus needs to be on the halting and circuitous process of learning to reach for the performative, for enactments of that which we profess as a matter of everyday practice.

Decentering requires an essay into the space in-between subject and subject, subject and subjectivity, subjectivity and subjectivity, where multiple, contradictory truths compose the landscape. This is the intellectual and spiritual space in which it is possible to learn to *care-in-action* rather than inuring ourselves to care by merely following the rules prescribed by common notions of civility.

Many of us fear the work of antiracism because we imagine that work in moral terms. If decentering calls us to a recognition of the ways in which we share beliefs, hope, and desire for racial justice with one another, across racial lines, it calls us also to recognition of the degree to which we are not yet (and may never be) free of racism. To the extent that decentering demands of us that we recognize, acknowledge, and account for the fact of racism as a composing force in our socially perceived identities as well as in our lived experience, it requires us to develop new ways of learning from and responding to those moments of failure in our performances of antiracism. Decentering demands of us that we learn from those moments when what we do, say, or write reveals our continuing struggle with indifference to those about whom we profess to care. Decentering demands of us that we acknowledge and learn from the ways in which our continuing struggles with whiteliness and internalized white supremacy or internalized racial oppression undermine our efforts to enact resistance to those forces.

When we think about antiracism in moral terms, we perceive its work as demanding adherence to universal principles of behavior and our failures to do so as catastrophic to our humanity. Within this field of reason, a true catastrophe becomes not just a possibility, but a probability. If antiracism is moral work and if it is true that we cannot simply, as an act of either desire or will, divest ourselves of our implicatedness in racism, then failure—the revelation of our indifference—is inevitable. We will, we know, be caught and outed as imposters, as knowing less than we have claimed to know, being less than we have claimed to be. And because morality cannot offer us ways of learning from these failures, these outings, or ways of recovering from them short of divine intervention, failure leaves us nothing to do but abandon the field.

Decentering, however, understood as an antiracist inquiry, is constituted by the search for and effort toward enactment of more fluid, context-driven, paradigmatic rather than rules-governed ways of knowing, being, and doing that characterize our treatment of those about whom we do, in fact, care. Decentering is an ethical practice employing *metis*: ways of knowing "emphasizing contingencies over essence, local [ways of knowing and being] over universal [principles or rules]" (Branch 2007, 207). The space in-between subject and subject, lived experience and lived experience, offers not a moral landscape but one which—because it is marked by paradox, excess, and transgression, because it is the place where things meet and intertwine with their opposites, because it is a mindscape within which we exceed our acknowledged definitions of self—we encounter the possibility of discerning and beginning to explore the dimensions of thicker relations. To conceive of the work of antiracism in these terms, as ongoing and processual, demanding not a rigid adherence to rules such that we prevent the possibility of either failure or surprise—the accidental revelation of indifference—but the engagement of dynamic and fluid, endlessly revisable practice, is to prise open the possibility of being ready for surprise: of learning the possibility of care in the borderlands. And in that place, failure, while painful and potentially shameful, is one of the ways in which care becomes both visible and possible.

Care or love (because we are talking about love, I think) conceived in the crucible of racial hegemony is easily emptied of meaning and easily subverted. To understand what happened between my brother and me, indeed to understand the complex tensions winding through multiracial relations and dialogues, and to understand what decentering might be and do in the context of antiracist activism, we must have language with which to name the intertwined forces of love and power. This is certainly true when what is the matter is personal, but it is also true as we seek to study and engage at the levels of systems and institutions. And we need this language also if we are to consider well and deeply the matter of antiracist epistemology and rhetoric. The forces of love and power so thoroughly infuse our everyday lives as raced subjects, whether we are conscious of them or not, that we cannot move mindfully unless and until we can offer an account of their interrelatedness, their interdependence, the ways and degrees to which they can either subvert or transform one another.

The antiracism activist movement, generally, is shaped and animated by sustained theorization and analyses of power. Antiracist activists are, of necessity, scholars of race and racism. In this context, we want to know what power is, how power works, and whether and in what ways we might be subject to it as individuals and as a collective. We want to know how power operates differently on different subjects and to what effect. And we want to know how to use power ethically, responsibly, and in transformative ways to work for a world more fully characterized by racial justice.

With Martin Luther King (and perhaps because of him), many antiracist activists are deeply influenced by theologian

Paul Tillich's account of power and its operations. Tillich defines power as desire and will, bound up with each other and exercised together toward self and collective realization or actualization (1960, 36–37). Further, Tillich asserts, power possesses two faces or aspects: one creative, constructive, and transformative, and the other conservative (in the sense of being preservationist), aggressive or coercive, and destructive. The first aspect of power Tillich terms *power-to*, and the second, *power-over*. Power-over is the act of preventing or thieving the self-realization of others (Kahane 2010, 263–68).

In this vein, antiracist activists tend to think and talk together about the power that names, defines, coerces, and constrains peoples of color—that oppresses, marginalizes, disenfranchises. We think and talk together also about the power that elevates and privileges whites over and against peoples of color, conferring advantages based not on the quality and value of labor and production by whites, but merely by virtue of being (or being perceived as being) white. Finally, we think and talk together about power that, by virtue of its predication in the logics of race and racism, and of white supremacy in particular, diminishes and dehumanizes all of us—prohibiting, in fact, the possibility of self and collective realization (Tri-Council Coordinating Commission 2004, sect. 1, p. 1). We are drawing on Tillich's work when we talk about power-over, making reference to a kind of three pronged process of power-in-action in which the effects of racism as oppression, racism as privilege, and racism as dehumanization overlap with, exploit, and magnify one another.

To understand and discern the usability of Tillich's conception of power-to, antiracist activists might also think and talk together about love and the complex relationship of love to power. As Tillich points out in his book *Love, Power, and Justice*, many of us are confused about this relationship. We tend to think of love and power as being inevitably in opposition to one another so that "love is identified with a resignation of power and power with a denial of love" (1960, 11). But for Tillich, love too is multifaceted, possessing both creative or transformative and destructive potential. Tillich defines love as "the drive toward the unity of the separated" (25). A few lines later, however, Tillich amends this definition of love not as the union of the strange, but "as the reunion of the estranged" (25). For Tillich, power and love are complementary: braided together and working in tandem they make one another generative (Kahane 2010, 180–183). Or, as Martin Luther King laid out the matter, "Power without love is reckless and abusive, and love without power is sentimental and anemic" (1967). The relationship between power and love might suggest to us—does, in fact, suggest to some antiracist activists—that we need to attend to needs and interests and differences on the one hand, and on the other to points of connection and resonance: to the joints, conjunctions, points of articulation between us (Kahane 2010, 198–200).

Similarly, though from a very different philosophical stance than Tillich's, in her book "Methodology of the Oppressed," Chela Sandoval writes of a "radical *mestizaje*[1] . . . understood as a complex kind of love in the postmodern world, where love is understood as affinity—alliance and affection across lines of difference that intersect both in and out of the body" (2000, 169). She contrasts this understanding of love with Barthes's account of "narrative love" composed around the singularity of a couple in love, situating *mestizaje* instead within the context of Barthes's conception of "prophetic love," which "undoes the 'one' that gathers the narrative, the couple, the race, into a singularity. Instead, prophetic love gathers up the *mezcla*, the mixture that lives through *differential movement* between possibilities of being" This love, writes Sandoval, is the "consciousness of the 'borderlands'" or "*la conciencia de la mestiza*"—not, in other words, love alone, but love that is both the location and the source of

---

1. Literally translated, *mestizaje* means "crossbreeding," "outbreeding," or "miscegenation." Here, Sandoval uses the term to refer to a conception of "joint kinship" defined not by bloodlines, but by "lines of affinity," occurring through "attraction, combination, and relation carved out of and in spite of difference" (2000, 168).

oppositional consciousness: the necessary condition for power-to (169).[2]

To practice decentering in this context intellectually and, I want to argue, spiritually, we must move, must reach or lean from the singular or narrative love, which we have learned is all there is of love, to a more capacious, more fluid love at the joint or hinge—to those very borders between ourselves and others where we have been estranged. Decentering requires of us that we learn to see ourselves and to be ourselves not in the kind of isolation from our relations with one another that permits the illusion of a natural, fixed, and stable self, but as unstable and unbalanced effects of those relations. When racism or whiteliness is at stake as a force separating and holding us fast in the singular, decentering can be painful. Moreover, decentering is always partial, always recursive, forever incomplete—a process rather than a destination at which any of us can claim to have arrived.

The invocation of terms like *love* and *power* in the antiracism movement can be confusing for a number of reasons. Both terms circulate widely in mainstream discourse and accrue multiple meanings within that discourse. Most of us, even when we have read and been influenced in a theoretical sense by the work of philosophers like Foucault and Althusser, are steeped in notions of power as exclusively coercive and love as fundamentally uncritical and certainly not oppositional. Further, the terms are easily and frequently conscripted in service not of personal and social transformation so much as the preservation of things as they are. In our quotidian lives, the exercise of power seems inevitably to involve abuse, and the exercise of love seems, albeit idealistically, to require unqualified affirmation. To think/speak/act, however, from an antiracist stance requires critical and oppositional engagement against the idea of whiteness and its rhetorical effects—against whiteliness. This necessity has been both misunderstood and misrepresented as

---

2. See also Anzaldúa (1999).

an opposition to whites as individuals. As such, it can seem or be represented as being antithetical to love. To recognize whiteness as an idea possessing a history and producing particular historical effects, however, should shift our analyses away from white supremacy as individual, aberrational behavior and toward a critique of whiteness as an ideological force that shapes individual and social consciousness—notions of the self as a body of lived experience and of the self in relation to the social—as subject.

To recognize whiteliness as a constellation of epistemological and rhetorical practices rather than an ontological condition of raced-white consciousness should shift our analyses as well as our actions away from moral binaries applied against the characters of individuals. Instead, such a recognition should direct us toward an evolving and collective critical awareness of the degree to which the quotidian ideological and rhetorical (re) invention of race and racism shapes what and how we come to know, what and how we speak and write, as well as the narratives of self we construct and perform as we learn, speak, and write across the range of contexts in which we act. Decentering, as an antiracist practice, does not obviate the necessary discernment of gaps or absences, the disjunctions, the failures of others' beliefs, arguments, or stories, but, paradoxically perhaps, has much more to do with the inward turn to become conscious of our own limitations or the degree to which we have internalized and reexternalized ideologies of singularity and separation. To engage in this work, we need to think carefully and critically about the ways in which notions of race, racial identity, and whiteliness have shaped who it is we think we are as activists, speakers, writers, or teachers as well as sisters or brothers, lovers, and friends.

Remember Flannery O'Connor's extraordinary short story, *Revelation*? The central figure is Mrs. Turpin, a round little white woman with "bright black eyes" who is, as the story begins, quite certain of and satisfied with her place in the world: her class position, her race, her faith tradition, her marriage, her relations within and to what she perceives as her community. The story begins with Mrs. Turpin's entrance into a doctor's office with her husband, Claud. And much of the story is taken up with Mrs. Turpin's gaze, as it were, at the other occupants of the doctor's waiting room and with the conversations and the subtext of the conversations she engages in with those Others. She notes the presence of a family she deems "white trash." She notes the presence of a "well-dressed, gray-haired lady" with whom she identifies and affiliates. Together, they talk across the surface and, implicitly, across the substance of their lives. They talk about work and families, about faith, and about their relationships with people of color who work for them or whom they encounter in other contexts in their daily lives. The ways and degrees to which Mrs. Turpin defines herself against these Others (white trash and people of color—to whom she refers using a particularly ugly racial epithet) become increasingly apparent. Most of the other characters in the waiting room seem also to be engaging in this means of self-definition and comfortable with this way of self-knowing.

As this conversation unfolds, however, Mrs. Turpin becomes aware that someone is gazing back at her and that this gaze is angry, enraged even. She becomes aware that her most mundane utterances—which she perceives to be comfortably, unquestionably true, *and virtuous*—are being scrutinized and found *lacking* or just downright *offensive*. The daughter of the gray-haired woman is staring at Mrs. Turpin with obvious malice. At some point, overcome by joy and gratitude for her position in life, Mrs. Turpin cries out in praise, "Oh thank you, Jesus, Jesus, thank you!" The daughter chooses this moment to wing her book at Mrs. Turpin's head and then to physically assault her. As you can imagine, chaos ensues, and the daughter is restrained then drugged. As the drug begins to work on her, the daughter raises herself up, looks at Mrs. Turpin one last time and says, "Go back to hell where you came from, you old wart hog." The daughter then slips into unconsciousness and is carted off to the mental hospital. Having seen the doctor, Mrs. Turpin and Claud return home.

Mrs. Turpin is deeply shaken by this encounter. Grappling with the memory of what has happened, Mrs. Turpin denies the accusation. "I am not a wart hog. From Hell." But, O'Connor writes, "The denial [holds] no force." Mrs. Turpin struggles with the fact that she, rather than the "trash in the room," has been singled out: not, she thinks, the "trash in the room," but Mrs. Turpin is singled out. A woman of faith whose certainty has been severely tested, she turns to God, now and perhaps for the first time, with doubt and anger. "What do you send me a message like that for?" she asks God. "How am I a hog and me both? How am I saved and from hell too? Why me? It's no trash around here, black or white, that I haven't given to. And break my back to the bone every day working. And do for the church. . . . How am I a hog? . . . Exactly how am I like them? There was plenty of trash there. It didn't have to be me." She cries out against God. "Who do you think you are?" And then, gazing at the sunset, Mrs. Turpin has a vision. She sees a "vast horde of souls" ascending to heaven. At the front of the line are the "white trash," "clean," O'Connor writes, "for the first time in their lives." And with them are the blacks and the wild-eyed, dancing and singing and laughing their way to heaven. Behind these are those with whom Mrs. Turpin would identify, "marching with great dignity, accountable," says O'Connor, "as they had always been for good order and common sense and respectable behavior." But Mrs. Turpin sees their faces, "shocked and altered," as "even their virtues were being burned away."

Flannery O'Connor's story ends here, with the revelation that the very virtues we good and well-intentioned whites hold most dear are those that we must lose, must burn away if we are to achieve unity with that which or the one(s) from whom we have been estranged. Readers are left to imagine what might come next for Mrs. Turpin—how she might choose to learn from, to deny, or to intentionally forget the revelation that has been given to her.

In the real world, though, the story rarely ends with the revelation, even, and perhaps especially, when we characters are most devastated by that which the revelation teaches. Even when we turn to denial or a willful loss of memory, the trace of the collision remains. Although the confrontation I described at the beginning of this chapter between my brother and me stands out from other, similar experiences by virtue of our closeness to one another and the depth and quality of our relations over time (all of my life and most of his), that February day was not my first experience of being called out and dressed down by a person of color or another white antiracist for my articulations, my performances of whiteliness, nor will it likely be the last. Such moments, I think, always provoke a crisis of identity, even when our first and only reaction to them is to contain and suppress their power in order to maintain the authority and legitimacy of our prior narratives, even in the face of the overwhelming challenge of an-Other. We have to work—hard—either to maintain ourselves as we would like to see and be seen as being, or to lean into that strange, terrible, and lovely Other story for the purposes of learning. We must choose the nature and quality of the labor in which we will engage and make this choice with recognition of the risks and obstacles attending either or both. To choose this labor and the learning it requires demands of us that we stay with and for one another even when staying is most difficult.

Mrs. Turpin's struggle, it seems to me, mirrors my own as well as the struggles of many white folks and predominantly white communities when we become aware of the critical gaze of the Other. We wrestle with the reality that contradictory truths about us, about how we come to know ourselves, about how we define ourselves, about how we act in and on the world, might be simultaneously true. The point is not that we have no virtues as individuals, that communities we create and sustain have no virtue. The point is that our virtues as individuals and our community virtues are mediated by race (as well as by other forms of identity). Our virtues are not fixed, settled, certain. And, in fact, our virtues are contested.

We are called to give an account of ourselves. It is possible to live without either hearing or heeding that call. Occasionally, however, if we are lucky, someone we love will throw a chair at us or something. And maybe in the exigency of a moment like this we are still capable of feeling the prick of need, of desire, as well as the uncertainty such moments engender: a sense of disorientation and loss—what Barthes refers to as the punctum: "that accident which pricks me (but also bruises me, is poignant to me)" (1980, 27).

The work of decentering as an antiracist inquiry engages us not in preparing to prevent the surprise and pain of these awakenings, but in cultivating a state of readiness and openness to the surprise of them. As much as such awakenings—emerging from perceiving and allowing oneself to be moved by accidents, by the prick and poignancy of the unexpected—may be disorienting, destabilizing, frightening, and risky, they are also threshold moments filled with hope and opportunity. The truth is that everyday antiracism across our institutions, and in communities across the country, is not, as we might tend to believe, revolutionary (in the sense of absolute rupture or an absolute overturning of existing systems of power and structure), not universally combative, not, typically transactional. Everyday antiracism is *slooow*, deliberative, reflective. Certainly everyday antiracism requires some courage, if for no other reason than that we are sure to make mistakes. In those moments when speaking truth to power is, in fact, what we must do, antiracism demands of us tremendous amounts of courage. And it is true that antiracism work is unsettling, in part, because of the ways it reveals to us the partiality of our self-knowledge.

When we become aware of how we may be seen by Others, how our actions—even and especially those actions we believe are most motivated by kindness and generosity—may be experienced as paternalistic or demeaning—as racist—we are called upon, as Mrs. Turpin was, to make sense somehow of being, at the same time, both virtuous and vicious, kind and mean spirited, generous and self-interested. The point of decentering as an antiracist inquiry is not to resolve these contradictions, but to grow from them an ethics of critical self-reflection, of care, and of engagement. The very partiality of our self-knowledge and our inability, frankly, to represent ourselves completely is precisely where that new ethics might begin.

Adorno has written, "We can probably say that moral questions have always arisen when moral norms of behavior have ceased to be self-evident and unquestioned in the life of a community" (quoted in Butler 2005, 3). Judith Butler explains that "Adorno refuses to mourn this loss, worrying that collective ethos is invariably a conservative one, which postulates a false unity that attempts to suppress the difficulty and discontinuity existing within any contemporary ethos. It is not that there was once a unity that subsequently has come apart, only that there was once an idealization, indeed, a nationalism, that is no longer credible, and ought not to be" (4). There is a sense in which the suggestion that there can be an absolute separation of our intellectual labor from the moral and ethical dimensions of our lives reflects a kind of conservative impulse. Just as our work always has a political dimension, so it also has moral and ethical dimensions. If we take seriously Margalit's distinction between morality and ethics, one of the ethical questions with which I think we are called to wrestle is how we whites will recognize, receive, and respond to interrogations of our most cherished notions about ourselves. How will we hear challenges to the work we do, that we most value, particularly when those interventions center around identity matters?

Our challenge is to conceive of an ethics of care that is broad, flexible, and open enough to allow not only for dissent, but for oppositionality. Meeting that challenge will require us, I think, to reconsider how it is that we confer and receive recognition. You will recall the certainty with which Mrs. Turpin reads the scene of the doctor's waiting room, the ways in which she names and in the naming reduces those who share the room with her to their membership in fixed and apparently stable, coherent categories: white trash; black; respectable. You might also recall the certainty with which I read the conditions of my brother's life and determined for him what he ought to do. In contrast to this kind of practice, Judith Butler advocates that we consider an alternative

> reading of the scene of recognition in which precisely my own opacity to myself occasions my capacity to confer a certain kind of recognition on others. It would be, perhaps, an ethics based on our shared, invariable, and partial blindness about ourselves. The recognition that one is, at every turn, not quite the same as how one presents oneself in the available discourse might imply, in turn, a certain patience with others that would suspend the demand that they be self-same at every moment. Suspending the demand for self-identity or, more particularly, for complete coherence seems to me to counter a certain ethical violence, which demands that we manifest and maintain self-identity at all times and require that others do the same. (2005, 41–42)

This new ethics might be driven in part by an awareness that there are innumerable standpoints from which to view the world, and by a recognition of the degree to which our own perspectives are limited and inadequate—that we need another point of view, to cop a line from a Victor Wooten song. Butler goes on, for example, to suggest that "one can give and take recognition only on the condition that one becomes disoriented from oneself by something which is not oneself, that one undergoes a de-centering and "fails to achieve self-identity" (2005, 42).

This may be as productive a way of thinking/becoming antiracist whites collectively as it is for each of us as individuals. How, I wonder, might our work be transformed if we are collectively willing to become disoriented, to engage decentering by inquiring in those moments when we are questioned, critiqued, or just nudged to see and do differently?

Decentering might be occasioned by those moments in our lives when the habitual fails us, when we are awakened to what we are doing and to who we are being by the accidental collision or confrontation between ourselves and Others. There is, however, something terribly wrong with waiting until someone you have wounded has thrown a chair at you to try a little decentering. We might choose and we might even posit that it is the responsibility of white antiracists to essay decentering less as an extraordinary epistemological and/or rhetorical practice of inquiry than as a daily discipline. This would mean, I think, working toward an everyday consciousness of the degree to which our representations of others and of self might be conditioned by learned and habitual ways of being and doing that are products of our own racialization.

Sometimes, when I am getting ready for work the way I do every day or driving a route that I follow every day, I suddenly experience this strange and shocking disorientation. Did I brush my teeth? I wonder. Or, did I just miss my turn? I do these things in a kind of semi consciousness such that I barely need to think at all; I am disassociated from the activity in which I am engaged until, by some accident, I am awakened. But I can try to stay awake. I can reach for a fuller consciousness.

What if we excavate our habitual inner dialogue, expose to ourselves, at least, the secret judgments we might be inclined to make, admit the secret biases that inform our interpretations and representations of one another and that perhaps impede our ability to listen mindfully when Others speak or write or even when conversations are overheard in passing. What if we attune to the mindlessness of our selves as we press the lock button on our car door as we drive through city streets, pull purses closer when in proximity to a man of color, begin reading the essay of a student of color with the expectation of finding error and learning little, congratulate colleagues of color on their articulateness, or pass over books written by scholars of color (especially when they address race in some way)?

But more than this, what if we attend to those moments when, inside our minds, we may be speaking over or interrupting others with the voice that by habit reads, sorts, and classifies others according to received, erroneous systems of inference. What if we inquire critically not only into the range of negative, demeaning, whitely judgments conditioned by internalized white supremacy or internalized racial oppression we might make as a matter of habit, but also into those judgments that confirm and affirm the narratives and performances of self and of others with whom we are inclined to feel some affinity by virtue of shared (or apparently shared) racial identity. What if we actively consider the nature of our inclinations to affiliate or to perform affiliation with others?

What if we acknowledge to ourselves if to no one else the privileges and benefits we do, in fact, enjoy by virtue of our whiteness and our consensual enactments of whiteliness? And what if we admit the extent to which those privileges and benefits are either unearned or earned in ways that, should we admit them, might make us burn with shame?

To take up the deep matter of internalized racial superiority, of internalized racial oppression, as well as of the profound differences in kind and degree of our awareness and resistance to these forces, is necessarily oppositional. Decentering inquiry presses the agon upon us, into us. The affective dimensions that accrue within the experience of this kind of inquiry are powerful and suppressive. This is why decentering, alone, is never enough in and of itself to constitute an antiracist stance or pedagogy. As a practice isolated from other antiracist practices, decentering can leave us with what we might be tempted to name as "feelings," but are really, I believe, the lived effects of ideologies of racial superiority and the materiality of internalized racial oppression—guilt, anger, a sense of immobility or helplessness; leaves us, in other words, with nowhere to move. Many whites are resistant to joining the antiracist activist movement because this sense of helplessness and hopelessness is the only experience they have had of the movement. In the face of these effects, they have left the field as many of us have been tempted to do without ever having learned the work beyond decentering.

The generative love and power that condition antiracism are not characterized by the absence of the agon register in our dialogues with one another, but by the ways in which activists, speakers, writers, listeners, readers engage with and perform within that register even as we reach for other registers. Decentering might be the opening move in antiracist dialogue. Beginning with a question, decentering demands of us the practice of postponement or stillness: the ability to listen and to intervene in the operations of that inner voice that judges, weighs, searches for gaps or absences too soon—the voice that seeks to expose and capitalize upon what it judges to be false by virtue of having uncritically projected or generalized lived experience onto the lives or narratives of Others. But in order to move, to shift, to reach still further toward the joint, the point of difference or separation between us, we need something more: to nuance not only what we see, hear, and feel, but how we come to make meaning of these senses. We need to study what one of my students termed the "connective tissue" between lived experience and individual memory, collective memory, and history. We need to learn to remember more and differently in order that we may narrate our racialization even, and especially within the agon register, in ways that support and sustain generative transracial love and enact the creative power of antiracism: the power to change the nature and quality of our relations both within and across racial lines. We need to learn the practice of transmemoration: of remembering without denying or effacing the memories of others and of situating our own and others' memories within the context of the collective—not just how *I* come to be, but how *we* come to be. This is the work of nuancing and is the subject of the next chapter.

4
ANGELS BEFORE THEE

Performative antiracism engages actors in forms of individual and individualized resistance—in work at the interior of one's self and one's affiliative relations with others. But performative antiracism demands more of us than this. Performative antiracism is labor that undoes the distinctions between personal and institutional, or systemic-change work. Antiracist actors work toward this undoing by uncovering and examining the living connective tissue between the ideas we hold—ideas that delineate the shape and quality of our relations—and ideas that delineate the deep or hidden racialized missions, structures, and practices of the systems, institutions, and social groups that enable and constrain our lives as raced subjects, as individuals, and as peoples. This practice of pursuing an idea, organizing concept, or belief both through its historical and intellectual genealogy, and through individual and collective memory and lived experience, is the practice of nuancing. Nuancing engages us in the work of recognizing and articulating critically the scope, dimensions, and impacts of existing relationships among and between the local and the global, the individual and the collective. But nuancing, as provisional and partial as the work must be, is also by design creative, critical, and generative. For nuancing, like decentering, contributes to the creation of new or transformed relationships among and between the local and the global, the individual and the collective.

Like decentering, nuancing is always, of necessity, processual and partial. We cannot gather up the whole of a matter for examination, particularly as we are in that matter and of it as well. Instead, nuancing involves taking a thin slice of what we see as an idea, concept, or belief that underpins a moment of relationship or a claim within an argument as we experience or observe it. Nuancing engages us in critical inquiry, but it is also a reflective practice in which we examine individual and collective memory to discern the impact of an idea, concept, or belief on our lived experience of the world and on the stories we tell about that lived experience. This double quality, or thinking-critically-at-the-joint quality, of nuancing—working in and out of intellectual, spiritual, social, and political histories while simultaneously working in and out of individual and collective memory—distinguishes nuancing from more traditional academic research and writing. Rather than excluding the *I*, nuancing scratches, teases, tears at the binaries between self and other, personal and social, subjective and objective, individual and collective.

Finally, we cannot practice nuancing well if we attempt it absent the ongoing work of decentering. Again, these practices are not stages we pass through, but ongoing and interconnected labors that attend one another. Decentering—the attempt at stillness, at postponement of judgment, at consciousness of bias, the reach not only toward empathy, but also and more so toward more just relations—is a necessary condition for the practice of nuancing. Decentering and nuancing are related practices in that both aim at undoing not the self qua self, but at undoing the idea of the self as distinct from the Other. They are not confessional practices aimed at achieving absolution, but practices of witness and testimony that connect ideas of the racialized self with histories and memories of that self's construction.

Nuancing intersects and in many ways coincides with the labor Krista Ratcliffe terms "rhetorical listening" and defines as "the performance of a person's conscious choice to assume an open stance in relation to any person, text, or culture" (2006, 26). Like rhetorical listening, nuancing is animated by the intentionality of its practitioners. As with rhetorical listening, nuancing is a profoundly political practice. Nuancing also proceeds from a logic of accountability, "invit[ing] us to consider how all of us are, at present, culturally implicated in the effects of the past . . . and, thus, accountable for what we do about situations now, even if we are not responsible for their origins" (32). Finally, nuancing, like rhetorical listening, engages practitioners in the analysis of cultural logics (and historical forces) out of which our claims about ourselves and the world are forged (33).

The differences between rhetorical listening and nuancing are largely rendered in the felt imperatives that drive them and the motivations that animate them as epistemological and rhetorical practices. Ratcliffe sees the purpose of rhetorical listening as "being to negotiate troubled identifications [with gender and race, including whiteness] in order to facilitate cross-cultural communication about any topic" (2006, 17). She sees rhetorical listening "as a response to [Jacqueline Jones] Royster's call for 'codes of cross-cultural conduct'" (17). These purposes, which are both necessary and laudable, should not be dismissed, but they are not the purposes of antiracist practice conceived either epistemologically or rhetorically.

As carefully and smartly as Ratcliffe articulates race as a socially constructed schema for perceiving and organizing human relations unequally along racial lines, the submersion of race within a cultural frame is not congruent with an antiracist analysis of race and racism,[1] the aim of which is not crosscultural communication, but the deconstruction of the logics of racism, the opposition to and dismantling of systemic and institutional racism. The aims of "negotiating troubled identifications" and "facilitating cross-cultural communication," I worry, are vulnerable to the same kind of critique Keith Gilyard mounts of calls for "multiracial tolerance and cooperation" (1999, 47). It is not enough, from an antiracist perspective, to offer an account of the degree to which race is "a social and rhetorical construction" (47) and to call, from within that construction, for the

---

1. See Introduction, pages 24–25.

negotiation of identifications and the facilitation of communication across those identifications. This is, I think, what Gilyard
means when he writes, hopefully, that "composition instruc-
tors—especially those who speak often of diversity and of getting students to understand, manipulate, or resist dominant discourses—will want to urge students to begin writing themselves
outside the prevailing discourse on race" (52). To do this work,
the antiracist work I hear Gilyard calling us to, we need to learn,
ourselves, in order that we might teach not how to function
within that prevailing discourse, but how to dis-function and,
by dis-functioning, to undermine and subvert its functionality—
the care and maintenance of racism itself.

Not surprisingly then, given the purposeful destabilization
and dis-functionality of antiracist epistemology and rhetoric, the
work of decentering and nuancing often is profoundly unsettling. These practices push us toward perspectives from which
those features of the stories we have been told and are inclined
to tell about ourselves and our places in the world appear no
longer as familiar, comfortable, and right, but as strange, unten-
able, and unavowable. With some regularity, I hear classroom
teachers and writing-center consultants express reluctance or
even fear at the idea of asking students to go to this narrative wilderness and to lose themselves as they know themselves
within it. Asking student-writers to engage reflectively and critically with race and racism produces anger, outrage, open hos-
tilities in the classroom and the writing center, they say. And, to
some extent, they are right. To some extent, it is not unreason-
able to be afraid.

I admit I am sometimes baffled by the depth and degree
of anger many white folks express when they are invited or
provoked to consider the matter of complicity with racism.
That is to say, I am baffled until I remember my own struggles
to remember, to acknowledge, to name, as well as the feelings of powerlessness with which I sometimes wrestle. When I
believe that the end of the work lies in the admission of guilt,
I too resist. But in as much as I am able to recognize that the

destructive power of racism extends far beyond what we as individuals do to one another, that the exercise of that power through systems and institutions possesses historical specificity, that I am capable of studying, analyzing, critiquing that destructive power not as a generalized, amorphous *thing* that is either too large or too small to account for, but in the particularities of its impacts, I am able to recognize also that the apportionment of blame is absurd on its face. The point of labors like nuancing, for whites in particular, is not to find oneself (or anyone else) guilty or innocent. The point is to transform the conditions of possibility for oneself *and* Others. Resistance to this work at some level, however, emerges from the conviction that, whatever any of us may say about the essay, the experiment, the attempt to decenter and to nuance, the labor for whites actually entails producing a predetermined, alternative master narrative that posits the actor/writer/speaker as racially (read inevitably) wrong. Beneath the anger of whites when invited to consider the dimensions and dynamics of racism, I think, lies a sense of helplessness: a conviction that the realization of wrongness is all there is and all there can be to the work.

It is true that as activists and teachers, writers, and speakers take up a labor like nuancing, we will be forced to abandon certain features of the narratives we construct about ourselves; features that we may, in fact, be very fond of; features that attend mythologies of the self as autonomous, self-sufficient, well intentioned (as if good intentions are all that matter), objective, qualified to judge, and good enough not to fear judgment. But running beneath these fears, in addition to (learned) helplessness, roils a different and much worse fear. Our recognition as raced subjects and, hence, the relationships we enjoy, relationships predicated on that recognition, are provisional. When we destabilize our racialization, make the processes and consequences of racialization visible and available for critique, we do, in fact, run the risk of becoming unrecognizable as raced subjects and, hence, as ones who can and ought to be loved, to those with whom we share racial identity and about whom we have tended to care most deeply. That is to say, we run the risk of being perceived as race traitors and thus not as unraced (which is often, in fact, the very condition nuancing critique calls into question), but as ones who transgress, who violate racial norms and the social positioning that attends those norms. We fear that we will be cast adrift and that our interest, our need for relationship, will be uncompleted. Many of us—particularly those of us who are peoples of color or who have grown up in multiracial affiliative relationships—have observed or experienced this slicing away or heard stories from our moms or dads, uncles or aunts, or grandparents about some form of this excision, and we *know* that what we fear is real.

If I didn't have children, I wouldn't have much of a social life outside my workplace. The truth is that I have never felt easy or comfortable in social gatherings. I don't know what to say to people at parties, and the result of my discomfort is that I end up talking a lot, but saying very little. Because I do have children, and because, oddly, given my own sedentary disposition, my children are quite athletic, I end up spending a lot of time not so much at parties as in ice rinks for hockey and figure-skating practices, lessons, tournaments, competitions, and shows. In the lobbies of the rinks I inhabit, there's a lot of chatter that goes on among parents—mostly (and irritatingly) about the children and whose is the most talented, most advanced, most elite of all. But occasionally, someone will ask me what I do and ask in such a way that I feel obliged to tell them about my areas of scholarship. If I tell folks that I teach writing and direct a writing center, almost invariably I am in for a long lecture on the illiteracy of kids these days, and nearly always when my interlocutors are white, an attending requiem on the death of rigorous public higher education caused by the lowering of standards that has attended the diversification of students attending colleges and universities. In these environments, when I say I study rhetorics of race and racism, there is another and related kind of catalog of responses I've learned to expect.

Peoples of color tend to express polite if reserved interest, in such a way as to suggest that they will wait to see what, if anything, might distinguish me from other white folks who profess opposition to racism while practicing what Vershawn Young, citing Derald Sue Wing et al. and Tim Wise, has termed the microaggression of Racism 2.0: the "mostly unintended 'racial slights and insults' . . . or enlightened exceptionalism, 'a form that allows for and even celebrates the achievements of individual persons of color'" (2010). But many white folks seem to feel a sudden need to discuss with me the ways in which they are not racist or to list for me the relationships they enjoy with peoples of color that certify their nonracist status. This conversation and its variations have played out for me so often that patterns have begun to emerge both in my responses to it and in what I hear (rather like listening to a piece of orchestral music so often you begin to hear it not only as a whole, but also as its strands or musical lines).

When the first disclaimer of racism or pronouncement of a certifying relationship with a person of color comes, I feel an ember of rage begin to glow in my belly. With that burn comes a self-check: is this not what I do when I think or talk about my relationship with my brother? I hold on to both the ember and the question. I split myself apart. Some of me is glazed over, appearing to be present and yet, inwardly, disassociated from the moment. I don't want to engage in the lobby of an ice rink with some parent or coach who will leave this conversation and go talk trash about me and my children across the room. Another part of me is parsing, trying to figure out some kind, compassionate, and critical way of saying back what I am hearing so the speaker might either shut up or get a clue. And some part of me is recording the conversation to reflect on later.

After years of these kinds of encounters, which, by the way, are not all that distinct from my conversations with many of my colleagues and students—though frequently those folks have more "sophisticated," read coded, ways of articulating their perspectives—I've come to this recognition: too many of us whitely folks look frantically for the rhetorical, the intellectual, the spiritual exit when race and racism become the subject of our conversation. And very often, that exit takes the form of an unexamined and rather superficial claim to a relationship or relationships that either legitimate the generalization of lived experience as a standard against which other lives, other lived experiences, might be measured and judged, or that justify the posture of innocence or noncomplicity. Too often, these conversations are nonperformative of antiracism inasmuch as they are taken as opportunities to affirm nonracism even as we think, speak, and do racism. It may be that there is a certain inevitability to this nonperformativity given the context in which such conversations tend to take place: not at the hearth, in intimate settings where we might confide some of the substance of our hearts and minds to one another, nor in the commons, where we come prepared to engage critically, intellectually with ideas and their histories.[2] No, these conversations occur in the superficiality of the casual, even accidental, encounter with one about whom it would be much more comfortable to assume thinks just as we do about the world and our place in it, but who, we discover, is strange and Other to us. In such moments, the rhetorical move of choice too often is the excision, the surgical separation, of oneself not only from the topic of conversation—race and racism—but also from oneself as a raced subject and, more critically, from the uncertainty, the blur, the murk of our relations with one another. Rather than deliberate, reflective attunement and engagement, we choose to absent ourselves from one another and from our collective memory and history.

My mom frequently advises me to "pick my battles." She tells me that I can't fight on every front, and she's right, of course.

---

2. In her book "Great Questions, Worthy Dreams," Sharon Daloz Parks describes three different kinds of conversations needed by traditionally aged college students and the spaces that seem to her to be generative of those conversations: table (where friends and family gather to break bread with one another and to speak with one another in intimate, but lively ways), hearth (that intimate space where a we might sit quietly with a trusted elder or friend), and commons (that public space wherein we gather to debate).

But to pick our battles well, we must have some set of principles and strategies by which we choose when to engage and how, and should be able to tell ourselves and one another the reasons we engage at any given moment, in any given context.

Very often, I know that my choice not to engage with a parent or coach, or with a colleague at work, or even with a student, is shaped by my desire to maintain some semblance of a relationship with that person and, perhaps even more so, with the community that person represents. In these moments, I am thinking first and foremost of myself and, at the rink, of my children. I am imagining the consequences of speaking out in interpersonal terms; my choice emerges from my concerns about the continuation and quality of relationships in a very localized sense. I am acting out of a learned vigilance—attending to that inner voice we have all acquired that schools me in the rules and conventions of *civil* discourse that constrains not only our most intimate relations, but also and more so, our relations with those about whom we know and seemingly care relatively little.

All of the antiracism training I've taken, all of the preparation for activist leadership and organizing I've undergone, does little to dampen that inner voice of vigilance or to ameliorate the guilt I feel when I choose not to engage. I tell myself that there are good reasons sometimes not to intervene, that sometimes the potential yield of interpersonal engagement is so small that the risks attending engagement aren't worth taking. I remind myself that my real work as an antiracist activist and educator extends far beyond those rather shallow and momentary relations with people who are passers-by in my life away from the classroom, the writing center, the university. When the person with whom I choose not to engage is a colleague or a student, I tell myself I can do more by cultivating this relationship and by choosing the time, place, and way to visit with them about race and racism. Or I tell myself, if the encounter has been particularly troubling, that I can do better by looking around for the community, institutional, or public support systems that enable and sustain the kind of racism I've heard articulated and working strategically to intervene there, in the company of allies.

And still I feel guilt. Still, I know that inner voice is working through me, however justified my choices may be, to maintain things as they are. And as I wrestle with that voice inside my head, long after the encounter that troubles me, my guilt morphs into a feeling, a sensation more complex, more strange, and more deeply wounding. I can call my friends and tell them, "You won't believe what so and so said!" "What an asshole!" I might say. And we can laugh together or console one another. I can apologize for my choice not to engage and move on from guilt. But this other feeling, this other sensation—it stays with me, haunts me. This other feeling, with its attending rush of heat that reddens my face, that tightens my muscles as if in readiness for collision or attack, that sends me tears of frustration and outrage: this feeling is, I think, shame.

Several years ago, I came across a YouTube video of an outtake from the movie *Derrida*, released in 2002. In this clip, Jacques Derrida talks about his fear of writing and describes that voice of vigilance in what I think is an extraordinarily apt way. Derrida acknowledges that, both in terms of its subject matter and in terms of how he writes, his scholarship can be perceived as "aggressive." He speaks of the fear that can attend producing such work. When he is writing, Derrida says, he does not feel this fear. He feels he is doing what must be done: writing what he writes and as he writes, of necessity. "Nothing," he says, "intimidates me as I write." But then, he continues,

> when I don't write there is a very strange moment when I go to sleep. When I have a nap and I fall asleep. At that moment in a sort of half sleep, all of a sudden I'm terrified by what I'm doing. And I tell myself, "You're crazy to write this!" "You're crazy to attack such a thing!" "You're crazy to criticize such and such a person." "You're crazy to contest such an authority, be it textual, institutional or personal." And there is a kind of panic in my subconscious. . . . In any case, in this half sleep I have the impression that I've done

something criminal, disgraceful, unavowable, that I shouldn't have done. And somebody is telling me, "But you're mad to have done that." And this is something I truly believe in my half sleep. And the implied command in this is "Stop everything! Take it back! Burn your papers!" "What you are doing is inadmissible!" But once I wake up, it's over. What this means or how I interpret this is that when I'm awake, conscious, working, in a certain way I am more unconscious than in my half sleep. When I'm in that half sleep there's a kind of vigilance that tells me the truth. First of all, it tells me that what I'm doing is very serious. But when I'm awake and working, this vigilance is actually asleep. It's not the stronger of the two. And so I do what must be done.[3]

Derrida's words move me. I recognize myself in them. And I recognize the complexity, the ambiguity, the contradictoriness of my own relationship to that inner voice of vigilance and to the feelings of shame that voice speaks out of and seeks to repress.

One of the most significant effects of whiteliness, as it works in and through us all across racial lines, is a state of demivolition, of demiconsciousness. And in that state, the vigilant voice, which polices *civil* discourse, is wide awake and possesses our ear. Of course my mother is right that we must pick our battles. But this powerful voice that speaks to us and through us when we are choosing what to say, to whom, and how, will not provide us with principled or ethical means of determining whether this is the appropriate or most strategic moment and way to engage. This voice lulls (or polices) us back to demivolition, demiconsciousness when it seems we may awaken, attend to the matter at hand wakefully, and perhaps *speak out*. This inner voice is an acquired one. We learn it at home, in classrooms, on the schoolyard—wherever and whenever we attempt to build relationships with others. In the acceptance we experience as well as through the rebuffs, the refusals of interest and lack of need for relationship with us, we acquire the voice that schools us. While it may

---

3. Jacques Derrida—Fear of writing. (n.d.), video clip, uploaded August 23, 2006, YouTube, http://www.youtube.com/watch?v=qoKnzsiR6Ss.

be that we can never unlearn this voice entirely—it will return to worry us when we sleep or when we move through the world of half sleep—we can learn to be conscious of its presence and impact on our habitual ways of being in the world. We can learn to resist this voice to the extent that we are able to study its history—to trace its origins, which are, in every case, both individual and social.

My brother was adopted by my parents in 1960. He was three years old. I was born two years later. Rick was born, my parents were told, on Red Lake Reservation in northern Minnesota, the eleventh child of a tribal member and a tribal police officer.[4] My brother is one of many generations of American Indian children whose removal from their homes, families, and tribes the U.S. government—in its efforts to eradicate all things Indian and, in fact, the Indian peoples from the face of the earth— advocated and sponsored. At birth, Rick was taken from his birth family and placed in foster care with a white family in a central Minnesota town. If my brother had been born after 1978, his removal from his birth family and any subsequent placement would have been subject to the Indian Child Welfare Act. He would not have been my brother.

My parents raised my brother, my sister (the oldest of us three and also adopted), and me in rural western Pennsylvania where they had found work as university professors at a small state university. Rural western Pennsylvania is an extraordinarily beautiful place. The northern reaches of the Appalachian mountain chain cut a great swath across western Pennsylvania. These rolling hills are covered in forest—pine, oak, maple, and low-growing primeval fern. And so in some sense our childhood was idyllic. We lived in the country—four miles from the closest town. We roamed freely, finding playgrounds not only in our

---

4. In some family stories, White Earth is the reservation on which Rick was born and, indeed, Rick's tribal membership is with the White Earth Tribe. It is clear to me from reading about the American Indian Adoption Project and the stories of American Indian children placed in white homes that the practice of dissembling both about tribal origins and family conditions was common among adoption agencies at the time.

own backyard, but also in the woods and hills that surrounded our home. But rural western Pennsylvania is also overwhelmingly and determinedly white. And as much as our lives were braided together by love of one another, they were cut through and through by racism.

Like other American Indian adoptees, however, strong the bonds of love bound us as a family, but within our home community Rick was cast always into perpetual strangeness and Otherness, and I, by extension, was cast as perpetual (condescending) stranger to my best friend. I remember the unspeakable sorrow attending my brother's recognition that no matter what he changed about himself (including how he spoke, read, wrote), he couldn't change his Indian-ness—that being white was not, for him, a possibility (he had already mastered the lesson that being white is desirable—the best that one could be). I also remember, quite honestly with a burning rage, the smug satisfaction of my parents' acquaintances as they acknowledged my parents' "generosity" in adopting my brother, saving him from a life of degradation and impoverishment inevitable, they thought, to children of the reservation.

In 1975, when I was thirteen years old and my brother was eighteen, we went together to a Halloween party at a KOA Campground outside of Knox, Pennsylvania (the town closest to our home). My dad had just bought my brother a little green Karman Ghia, a classic car of which my brother was incredibly proud. We drove to the party in that car. We hadn't been there very long when a crowd of football players from our school arrived. One of these young men, the son of one of our parents' colleagues at the university, entered the clubhouse wearing a Ku Klux Klan costume; he had painted the words "Kill the Nigs" on the front of his robe. My brother confronted this young man and a fight broke out. I remember moving outside and struggling through a crowd of bat- and crowbar-wielding men—some of high-school age and others older, all drunk. I remember screaming at them to leave my brother alone. I remember my arms being pinned behind me and sweaty white faces distorted by rage. I remember the words, "He's not your brother, he's a fucking nigger." I remember seeing my brother, bruised and bloody, watching his car being destroyed by the mob. Someone—I can't remember whether it was me or not—called a family friend who came to get me. I think one of Rick's friends helped him to escape the crowd. The family friend thinks he may have driven my brother's car back to our home that night. My mom thinks the car wasn't driveable and that it was towed home the next day. Someone else, my father maybe, parked or had the car parked in our backyard and there it sat, rotting, for years—a mute testament to yet another violent eruption of the hatred in our community for my brother, and also for the kind of family we were.

The year was 1975. The civil rights movement was on the wane. Rick and I had been too young to take in the events of the period. I had been three and he had been eight when protestors marched on Montgomery and were stopped and beaten at a police blockade on the Pettus Bridge. I was six and he was eleven when Martin Luther King was murdered. We didn't understand the significance of the demonstrations, the violence that attended the suppression of those protests, or of the Supreme Court decisions, or of the legislation that was passed during our childhood: the Civil Rights Acts of 1964 and '68 and voting rights legislation. But the stories of these events, the stories of the heroism of civil rights activists—of James Chaney, Andrew Goodman, and Michael Schwerner, of Medgar Evers, of King and Malcolm, and of the members of the Black Panther Party—these stories lived in our imaginations.

We had grown up around a dining-room table where the stories of a civil rights revolution were told, threshed through, where racial oppression was decried and the successes of the movement celebrated. These stories ran side by side in our imaginations with stories from movies of the era. I was too young to see *Shaft*, but I remember that my brother was allowed to go to the movie, an experience that profoundly impacted both his sense of himself in the world and his tastes in fashion. Both of us watched *The Trial of Billy Jack*, and however awful the film might have been for film critics, for us it was epiphanic. We wanted to be that guy. We didn't understand at the time that these films, while ostensibly celebrating black power and the American Indian movement, reified racist tropes and stereotypes, evacuating, in the popular imagination and in public discourse, the social movements of the 1960s and early '70s of their radical character and their liberatory potential.

Two years previously, in 1973, alongside the nation, my brother and I had watched the television news as American Indian movement members, at the request of traditional chiefs on the Pine Ridge Reservation in South Dakota, had taken over and occupied the town of Wounded Knee for seventy-one days before a negotiated end to the standoff was reached. The stakes in the occupation were both high and complex. Most immediately, tribal elders sought the removal of Tribal Chairman Dick Wilson, an assimilated Lakota whose administration was backed by the Bureau of Indian Affairs. Wilson's leadership of the tribe was dictatorial by nearly all accounts. He oversaw a campaign of terror and intimidation aimed at traditional tribal members who continued to speak Lakota, to practice traditional medicine, and to worship in traditional ways. Wilson and his goon squad worked to ensure that members of the tribe who chose not to assimilate were severely punished through the withholding of food, education, and jobs, but also through ongoing and systematic violence against them. But the tribal elders and the AIM leadership sought justice also in the long and terrible matter of treaties made and broken by the U.S. government (Grimberg et al. 2009).[5]

Following the end of the occupation, AIM leaders travelled to Washington DC to meet with White House officials as per their negotiated agreements. One meeting occurred during which those officials refused to honor the agreements made at Wounded Knee, and AIM leader Russell Means was arrested and imprisoned. During the standoff at Wounded Knee, the federal

---

5. See also Treaty of Fort Laramie with Sioux, etc. 1851, and Treaty with the Sioux: Brule, Oglala, Miniconjou, Yanktonai, Hunkpapa, Blackfeet, Cuthead, Two Kettle, Sans Arcs, Santee, and Arapahoe 1868.

government fired 500,000 rounds of ammunition into the town. Two Indians were killed by government forces and one FBI agent died in the fighting as well.[6] The Indians at Wounded Knee were heroes in our eyes and yet we knew so little about them and still less about the ways their lives, their everyday experiences of racism, connected with Rick's, with mine, with our family's very existence.

Residents of Pine Ridge Reservation refer to the years between 1973 and 1976 as the Reign of Terror. During that time, Dick Wilson exacted a terrible vengeance upon tribal members who had participated in or supported the occupation at Wounded Knee. During these years, thanks largely to Wilson's violent regime, the reservation suffered the highest murder rate per capita in the nation. Finally, in June 1975, two FBI agents were killed on Jumping Bull Ranch on the Pine Ridge Reservation when they attempted to enter the property where AIM members had been invited to stay under the protection of elders there. But this part of the story we heard little about.

We had watched, we had listened, and what we saw and heard fired our imaginations. But there were these vast and utter silences that also shaped our understanding. We lived double lives. At home, around our dining-room table, the stories were told, but their significance, their relevance to our own immediate lived experience, went unremarked. We lived in a community relatively untouched either by the social turmoil of the civil rights movement or by the changes that movement wrought. We lived as a family whose very existence, in the most literal sense, had been made possible by the fact of racism; we were exposed to and subject to racism daily. And yet none of us ever connected either the everydayness of that racism or the events of that terrible Halloween night with the history we were living. We knew about racism, theoretically, and yet, to the best of my knowledge, we never, ever talked as a family about the racism around us as *racism*.

---

6. For more history of the Wounded Knee Occupation and events on Jumping Bull Ranch, see Matthiessen (1992).

I ask my mom over and over again about that night and the weeks that followed. "Did you ever talk to that guy's parents?" I want to know. "Did you talk to the school?" I was a year younger, in 1975, than my son is now. I imagine myself in full-blown Mama-Bear mode, blasting my way through police stations, his school, in meetings with parents. "If it were my son . . ." I think. I don't remember anyone ever talking with me about what I had witnessed or how I felt about what happened. "Did you ever talk with Rick?" I want to know. She tells me my dad was most upset about the damage to the car, which was too extensive to ever be repaired. One day when I ask, she tells me she had a meeting with the vice principal of our school, but a week or so later, she reminds me of the rest of the story.

The following week, Rick and I went back to school and, although rumors flew among our classmates about the fight at the KOA, we remained silent. We pretended as if nothing had happened until one afternoon. I had just taken my seat in my general business class when a friend came running into the classroom to tell me that my brother was beating the living daylights out of someone in the boys' bathroom. With my teacher hollering behind me to take my seat, I shot up and out into the hallway. I'm not sure what I intended as I headed for the fight. I think I wanted it to be fair. If Rick was in for another mobbing, I wanted to be there with him, fighting on his side. Before I reached the restroom, though, Rick strode out through the door. His nose was bleeding a little, but his head was high and his eyes were on fire. They rested on me just for a moment and then he was gone. He had entered the bathroom and found himself alone in there with the football player who had come to that party in KKK robes. Rick had confronted him again and fought him one on one; and Rick had won. I was jubilant! Rick had taken some of his own back, I thought. He had fought back. And he had won! I turned to follow him and came face to face with the vice principal, Mr. Cunningham. I yelled at him. "Don't you go after my brother. That fucking asshole . . ." and I was off—yelling the story at him, justifying my brother's participation in the fight while other students stood by listening, impressed more by the array of swear words I employed in telling the story to an authority figure than with the story itself. Mr. Cunningham told me to settle down and go back to class. My mom says she had a meeting with him the following day. "Don't you punish my son," she remembers saying. "He was provoked." I smile as she tells me this. I can't help myself. "Provoked," I think. That's one way of putting it. Mr. Cunningham, she says, told her, "Don't worry, Ma'am." And nothing more was said. Nothing.

Like far too many of his generation and of the generations that preceded his—like many of the men and women who gathered in solidarity with tribal elders at Wounded Knee— my brother was taken, stolen. Many among Rick's generation and those who came before had survived the Indian boarding schools and the Indian Relocation Program, which aimed to move Indian families away from their reservations and to assimilate them into white society in cities across the country. As an American Indian adoptee, Rick's experience was different from and yet contiguous with theirs. As whites who participated, wittingly or not, with good intentions or not, in the removal of Indian children from their families and communities of birth, my mother's, my father's, my sister's, and my experiences were also different from but contiguous with those of other whites who took part in or stood by and watched the dismantling of Indian families and communities.

Sir James Fraser, whose stories in *The Golden Bough* became fodder for Rick's and my imaginative play as children, wrote in a footnote, "Unless we allow for [the] innate capacity of the human mind to entertain contradictory beliefs at the same time, we shall in vain attempt to understand the history of thought in general and of religion in particular" (1935, 5). Our lives, as members of a multiracial family forged by force and also welded together by love, were fundamentally contradictory. But that contradictoriness is not now and was not then unique to our everyday experience, but inherent to the historical, social processes of racialization and racial formation.

In their book *Racial Formation in the United States from the 1960s to the 1990s*, Michael Omi and Howard Winant write that "racial formation is a process of historically situated *projects* in which human bodies and social structures are represented and organized" (1994, 55–56; italics in original). The processes of racialization and racial formation, Omi and Winant continue, occur

> through a linkage between structure and representation. Racial projects do the ideological "work" of making these links. *A racial project is simultaneously an interpretation, representation, or explanation of racial dynamics, and an effort to reorganize and redistribute resources along particular racial lines.* Racial projects connect what race *means* in a particular discursive practice and the ways in which both social structures and everyday experiences are racially *organized*, based upon that meaning. (56; italics in original)

The American Indian Adoption Project alongside the American Indian boarding school movement, and the American Indian Relocation Program, are interrelated examples of a racial project that worked both to explain and justify not only the utter domination, but the near genocide of American Indians. Practically speaking, they were also and simultaneously logical extensions of the genocidal project. These programs both depended and capitalized upon representations of American Indians—regardless of tribal affiliation and spiritual traditions, regardless of political and social organization within the tribes—as savage, uncivilized, unwashed, murderous, duplicitous, manipulative, sly, wild and free, but also, and sadly, peoples of a past gone for good. These programs were designed to facilitate the "progress" (read annihilation) of Indian peoples from this racial state of being to a whitely state of being—never fully white, of course, but assimilated within white society and culture.

Even as large or macroscale racial projects link representations of raced bodies to structures of social organization, situating both representation and structure within racial hegemonies, they also operate at the microsocial level to handcuff individual and collective lived experience of racial formation to what passes for "common sense" (Omi and Winant 1994, 59). "Everybody learns," Omi and Winant write, "some combination, some version, of the rules of racial classification, and of her own racial identity, often without obvious teaching or conscious inculcation. Thus are we inserted in a comprehensively racialized social structure" (60). Racial formation in the United States works in and through us so we are always attuned to race and schooled either to be unconscious of that attunement or, if we are conscious of it, schooled to expect stringent consequences for naming what we see, feel, know of it.

For me, the events of that Halloween night have taken on, I realize, a kind of metonymic quality in my memory and in my imagination. They stand in for hundreds of everyday experiences of racial aggression, disciplining, schooling in the racial rules: for the cruel words of children tossed about on daily school bus rides to and from school; for refusals of friendship on the playground and in the hallways of school; for the indifference or outright hostility of teachers; for the lies published in textbooks we were forced to read and then tested on; for all of the rejection, the bullying; for all of the hardness of hearts and minds. I wonder, but cannot discern, what might have been different for Rick and me, for all of us, if any of us had been able to see and to talk together about the ways our everyday experiences or the violence of that Halloween night were connected philosophically, logically, ethically, politically to the events we had watched unfolding on television: the repression, the demonstrations, the speeches, the changes in law, and the ways a shaken world tends to settle back into stasis.

I wonder, but cannot know, whether things would have been different for Rick and, truth be told, for me as well if we had been sponsored, provided with the necessary intellectual and spiritual scaffolding, and authorized to name the racism that ran us through as *racism*. Our parents, our school, our community were caught in the same dynamic complexity, the same web of contradiction we were. In particular, despite our parents' credentials as scholars, despite their liberal to left politics, despite their deep and abiding love for us, and despite the historical moment that framed our childhood, they, and thus we, had no way of fighting back that might have yielded something more than a pyrrhic victory in a bathroom brawl. Unconnected from the ongoing, collective struggle for racial justice, absent the collective will of other peoples of color and of antiracist whites to ally with my brother against racism in our community, the events of that autumn stood in fact and in memory as uncontested aberrations in an otherwise relatively untroubled racial order. And that wicked whispering voice echoed down the years: "He's not your brother; he's a fucking nigger."

Racial violence, like other forms of discipline and punishment, always possesses this double-edged quality. Whether physical or psychological or symbolic, whether practiced as threat or materially enacted, whether carried out by individuals or by mobs and/or by institutions and the systems whose interests are served by those institutions, racial violence works over and against peoples of color and whites as both retribution for and deterrence against transgressions of the rules of racial standing. That is, the effect of racism is, on one hand, to communicate and to enforce a repressive racial order over and against people of color. This is true not only of the most explicit and violent forms of racism—lynching, for example—but also of more implicit, more coded forms of institutional racism, such as the generalized attachment of moral turpitude to students of color and their families when they fail to "succeed" in classrooms and on standardized tests that, by design, work to their educational disadvantage. Racism also, on the other hand, communicates to white folks the contingent or conditional nature of our racial identity and of our acceptance or inclusion within white families and communities, within the white-dominated social order. All of us—peoples of color and whites—are schooled by racism in all of its forms as to who we are or may be authorized to become, in the racial rules by which we must abide by virtue of our racial assignations, and in the various consequences that will attend transgressing racial order.

There are a number of means by which a racist racial order is maintained. Some of those means are designed to preserve class assignations, for example, and some are aimed at the conservation of political capital and power. Other means are focused on careful control of the mechanisms for the legitimation of thought and discourse, of epistemologies, rhetorics, and discursive registers.

The policing of individual and collective memory, of history, and of the discursive registers through which memory and history may be articulated and authorized, is a critical operation in the maintenance of an apparent equilibrium within, among, and between the self and the web of systems and institutions enabling and constraining individual and collective consciousness and agency. The policing of language and the circumscription of "legitimate" and "intelligible" discourses for the production of new knowledge and understanding is another such critical operation. The application of the logics of individualism to the social, systemic problem of racism is yet another critical operation. Here, meaningful, productive, performative dialogue is prevented through the continual enforcement of the logics of blame apportionment, of individual notions of accountability, and through the ongoing valuation of conservative or traditional forms of retributive justice. Taken together, these mechanisms effectively prohibit resisting ideation and knowledge production as well as performative antiracist discourse. Nuancing is one means, albeit partial, processual, and recursive, of taking on these mechanisms, making them visible and audible, available for critique, and for revealing the instability of social relations they aim to occlude.

Here are some of the suppositions and conditions nuancing might be used to expose and subvert:

THE AGON

Many of us have been well schooled in the rhetorical arts of speaking and writing to win—to defeat or eliminate an opponent and/or an opposing argument. Perhaps we have learned to conceive of winning as achieving a good grade, or have come to see winning as achieving the silencing of an Other, getting in the last word, or accomplishing the rhetorical knockout by mounting an argument that is somehow unassailable. Maybe we've learned to see winning as successfully mounting and crafting an argument that is legitimate by virtue of the coherence of its appeals, that effectively resolves or disguises contradiction. Too many of us have been taught and have passed on to others our learned conviction that references to one's self, one's perspectives, one's memories, are "personal" and, hence, anti-intellectual. In so doing, we have, in fact, actively prevented ourselves and others from undertaking intellectual and rhetorical work far more difficult and rigorous than what we might think of as traditional argument. We have actively prevented ourselves and others from gaining access to critical epistemologies and rhetorics that collectively possess far greater use value in both individual and collective senses for performative antiracism, at least. In contrast to traditional argument, nuancing should be aimed not at foreclosing ongoing conversation, but at inviting greater participation. Nuancing ought not conclude, but incite, provoke, and welcome addition, intervention, complication, and the conjoinment of Other articulations.

In his book *Beclouded Visions: Hiroshima-Nagasaki and the Art of Witness*, Kyo Maclear suggests a critical distinction in the practices of remembering between *commemoration* and *transmemoration*. While commemoration invokes notions of remembering as a unifying practice, transmemoration, Maclear notes, "signals a coming to terms (to language) with the ways in which our identities and understandings are unevenly implicated in wider social and symbolic formations structured on power and inequality" (1998, 155). Nuancing takes up the labor of transmemoration and, as it does so, suggests an alternative ethics—less characterized by claims of common ideals or universally good ways of being and doing in the world than by a concern with "the kind of person one must become in order to establish a nonviolative relationship to the other" (Cornell quoted in Maclear, 155) "An ethical relation," Maclear writes, "assumes a commitment to 'guard' otherness 'against the appropriation that would deny

her difference and singularity'" (155). Nuancing, as an antiracist practice, as a range of rhetorical moves and communica-
tive acts, presses against traditional notions of logos and ethos.
It is far less a rhetoric designed for defeating the arguments of
others by asserting inarguable reasoning from an unassailable
position than for speaking and writing of race matters so others
may join the conversation and the conversation might continue
infinitely (Carse 1986, 3).

WHITELINESS

Most of us have been taught and have passed the lesson on that
if peoples of color wish to intercede in the unequal distribution of power, access, equality, and justice, they must not only
acquire fluency in but also master a particular kind of English,
and by extension a particular and whitely kind of rhetoric.
Stanley Fish makes this argument when he suggests that the use
of Englishes other than "standard" or academic English creates
the conditions for the enactment of racism. "You're not going
to be able to change the world," Fish writes, "if you are not
equipped with the tools that speak to its present condition. You
don't strike a blow against a power structure by making yourself
vulnerable to its prejudices."[7]

In a brilliant critique of this position (for which Fish is merely
a mouthpiece), however, Vershawn Young and Aja A. Martinez
point out that language discrimination is an effect of racism
and not it's cause. They suggest firstly that Fish's argument rests
on the false assumption that the "dialects" of those who would
intercede are inadequate, impoverished, and incapable of the
intellectual and critical weight necessary to engage productively with and against systems of power and privilege. Secondly,
Young and Martinez point out that Fish has also argued that
those who have mastered "standard" English have learned
enough to know that the language doesn't need intervention

---

7. Stanley Fish. What should colleges teach. Part 3, *Opinionator* (blog),
New York Times, September 7, 2009, http:opinionator.blogs.nytimes.
com/2009/09/07/what-should-colleges-teach-part-3.

or intercession. And, finally, Young and Martinez argue that even as Fish suggests that the best way to change a system is to be a part of it, he uses peoples of color who have succeeded and advanced within the existing system as examples of how well that system works (2011, v). Young and Martinez point out our collective hypocrisy when they write:

> Too many of us double-speak, claiming out one cheek that varieties of English are fully compatible with and sometimes more expressive than standard English. Out the other cheek we say, "But students must master the rules of standard English usage for standardized tests, to show that they can be successful as professionals at work, and at various stages of school." "Our hands are tied," some of us say. We then close our eyes as we tie many of our students' tongues, in hopes that a few will be successful, while knowing from history, past experience, and current statistics that most don't succeed, certainly most people classified as minorities won't, not under the current limited rubric of what counts as linguistic success. (vii)

Young and Martinez, alongside the scholars whose work is represented in their edited collection, argue for learning and teaching a principled linguistic copia,[8] or expansiveness and abundance: a practice Young has termed "code meshing." Similarly, nuancing engages its rhetors in a kind of rhetorical copia. As a range of rhetorical practices, nuancing interrelates with code meshing by cultivating and valuing the abilities of speakers/writers to move fluidly between Englishes and rhetorical modes within a text or utterance.[9]

---

8. My good friend Rex Veeder reintroduced me to this term in the summer of 2010 in private conversation and correspondence. Professor Veeder's current work with the concept centers around the blues, healing heart and mind, and labors for social justice.

9. Young's work provides excellent examples of both code meshing and nuancing as well as of the relationship between the two in both principle and practice. See for example *Your Average Nigga: Performing Race, Literacy, and Masculinity* and "Momma's Memories and the New Equality."

DISINTEREST AND "OBJECTIVITY"

Many of us have been taught and have passed on the erroneous lesson that one can mount an argument that is objectively true, that is unimplicated in the wash of the social, the political, the historical—of power—over and through us all. We have been taught and passed on the lesson that to argue any other way than "objectively" (where the meaning of objectivity is sharply circumscribed by whiteliness) is to argue illogically. We have, in other words, invested disinterestedness with the properties of reason. We have been taught that interested arguments are transgressive—in the sense of revealing more about the self than one's readers would ever need or want to know—or just plain rude—speaking and writing in ways that offend the codes of civility governing communication among a community of citizens, colleagues, or scholars.

But there is more. For we have also assigned particular meaning and significance to the performance of argument unequally along racial lines. As Gerald Graff notes in his chapter, "Code Meshing Meets Teaching the Conflicts," students of color are often actively discouraged from engaging in vigorous debate. "If anything," Graff writes, "schools steer away from controversy, motivated no doubt by the fear that verbal argument can get out of control and escalate into violence. Instead of seeing children's argumentative skills as a resource to be cultivated and built on, then, schools often discourage argumentative students or stigmatize them as troublemakers" (2011, 101). It is worth noting the racist stereotype implicit in the belief that peoples of color engaging in vigorous debate are likely to turn violent as well as the racism implicit in the practice of denying literacy education, generally, and instruction in rhetoric, in particular, to students of color based on that stereotype. Too many of us in both academic and public domains have insisted that, on the one hand, to speak and write well within the academy or within the professions, peoples of color must join as skilled rhetors in ongoing debate, and, on the other hand, have stigmatized their possession of rhetorical skill, responding to it with fear and resentment rather than engagement. Further, we have stipulated the conditions for entering those debates in ways that systematically advantage and disadvantage rhetors along racial lines.

Nuancing as a range of antiracist rhetorical practices provides speakers and writers with both structure and support for naming, examining, and intervening productively in the construction of self and conception of Other as raced subjects contending with race matters. Nuancing, at its best, should enable its rhetors to cultivate a critical awareness of the complex and dynamic relationship between the self and the social, the self and the historical production of raced subjects. As a range of ethical practices—or an ethos—nuancing should give antiracist rhetors a means to name and engage critically with the question of what to do and how to both singly and together reshape relations within and across racial lines.

WHITE GUILT

Many of us have been taught and have passed on the lesson that any discussion of race and racism is always also a discussion aimed at the assignation of blame and the determination of guilt. We have learned and passed on the erroneous notion that antiracist epistemology and rhetoric are animated by a fundamental punitive impulse. The prevalence of the logics of retributive justice across a vast range of social contexts leads whites to infer that any discussion of racism must be motivated by a desire or need to punish. The range of epistemological and rhetorical moves within these logics is restricted to those that establish and assert the guilt or innocence of individuals.

In this context, among the catalog of reasons any of us might offer for not taking up race matters within our communities, our families, our classrooms, one of the most prevalent and powerful narratives has to do with how uncomfortable, how angry, discussions about race and racism seem to make white people feel. We doubt our ability to engage in meaningful conversation about race and racism productively, but we doubt even more the ability of other whites to hear and to attend to what we have to say. We are afraid we will be unable to contain and manage the range and depth of feelings such conversations might engender. We worry about the convictions of whites that such conversations are designed to humiliate and blame them for matters that seem to them to be beyond their control. Nuancing, however, should, help us dis-articulate guilt from shame. Nuancing should help us distinguish, in other words, individual responsibility for causing harm to an Other and for profiting from that harm from the individually experienced affective dimensions—the shame—of remembering and acknowledging the force of racism in our lives. Nuancing should help us recognize the depth of our need and desire for relationship with those from whom racism has estranged us.

In her book *Blush: Faces of Shame,* Elspeth Probyn draws on prior work by Sylvan Tomkins to theorize shame as an affect dependent on interest or care. "If you don't care," writes Probyn, "then attempts to shame won't move you" (2005, x). "Shame," she suggests, "illuminates our intense attachment to the world, our desire to be connected with others, and the knowledge that, as merely human, we will sometimes fail in our attempts to maintain those connections" (14).

For Probyn (and for me), shame is quite distinct from feelings of guilt. The latter, Probyn argues, are passing senses—the affective remnants of having erred such that one might simply apologize and move on. "Guilt," she suggests, "is easier to get rid of [than shame] and once dealt with is forgotten, whereas shame lingers deep within the self. . . . Shame makes us quiver" (2). To put the difference another way, guilt is an affect that attends the abridgement or compression of interest. Shame amplifies care or interest such that we experience a cascade of affects or feelings (depending on one's philosophical or disciplinary orientation); shame beckons us and demands that we come to what Probyn terms "propriocentrism," or awareness of the extent and degree to which the affects or feelings that attend shame are related to and/or interconnected with one another. "Guilt," she writes, "makes no demands for such a 'theory of minding:' a means by which we might determine the relative importance of multiple affects" (2005, 23). Guilt is the progenitor of the vigilant voices that urge us toward demiconsciousness, that maintain our participation in the consensual hallucination that what is at stake is who's to blame rather than what to do. Guilt enforces the silence of denial and speaks most forcefully through that silence. Guilt locates us within the social force of racism even as it forces denial from our lips. Shame, in contrast, calls our attention to the possibility or actuality of unbelonging, of in-betweenness, or of "being out of place" (xvi). Shame forces us to notice not only our yearning for relationships with one another across racial lines, but also the degree to which our sense of our own humanity is contingent upon the degree to which others recognize us not only as human, but as worthy of their care. Nuancing presses us to write out of and back to this recognition—to write for one another from the state of in-betweenness, of out-of-placeness.

At its best, nuancing is a practice that enables its practitioners in successive and processual turns to notice the internal and external vigilant voices as well as the silences that are an effect of guilt logic, not as articulations of the familiar or the "commonsense," but as strange and intrusive—worthy of study, in other words. Nuancing should both call on and enable us to attend to those voices by historicizing them and coming to recognition of them as ideologically imbued: as functions of ideologies that not only legitimate, but institute racism (whether or not minding them at any given moment seems an appropriate strategic decision).[10] By situating what and how those voices and silences speak within the social, the historical, and the ideological, rather than within individual and aberrational discursive fields, nuancing might help all of us to understand the ways and degrees to which the ideological work those voices of vigilance

10. For an excellent exposition of this understanding of ideology, see for example *Mapping the Language of Racism: Discourse and the Legitimation of Exploitation* by Margaret Wetherell and Jonathan Potter.

and vigilant silences preserve things-as-they-are by threatening the apportionment of blame along individual lines. Nuancing should give us means of recognizing, making sense of, and attending to the critical differences between guilt understood as the acceptance of fault or blame, and shame understood as the incompletion of interest and need, as an affective experience of the relational prohibitions—the rules of racial standing—that attend institutional and systemic racism.

FEAR

Many of us worry about the pain that may be inflicted upon peoples of color who must listen to the expressions of white privilege, resistance, and outrage within multiracial contexts where race is not only at the table, but where its presence is also acknowledged. At some level, these fears are, I think, quite legitimate and critical to consider if we are to act well and ethically. Perhaps such fears are so legitimate that more of us should feel them. We do need to consider with and for whom we are speaking or writing.

But we may also need to recognize the degree to which these kinds of fears are effects of racism, itself. Perhaps we need to probe the question of whether, how, and to what degree the fear of hurting peoples of color by speaking openly and critically of race and racism are expressions of whitely paternalism conditioned by implicit convictions about the weakness and vulnerability of peoples of color. Peoples of color tend, in fact, to have a more sophisticated and nuanced understanding of race and racism than whites. This may be so because very often peoples of color live in conditions that demand their attention to race matters on a daily basis in ways that whites simply do not experience. The greater danger, I think, is that we will attend to race matters in either public or academic contexts in ways that orient toward whites, in effect recentering whiteness. The greater danger, I think, is that we will continue (for this is, too often, what we already do) to practice antiracism nonperformatively: that we will continue to place peoples of color in the position of having to bear witness in endless reiterations to this recentering or, relatedly, that we will continue turning and returning to peoples of color with the expectation that they will teach us about race matters. These are the kinds of conditions that enjoin silence-as-absence.

Another fear we may feel about initiating or joining in multiracial discussions of race and racism, in particular, is the possibility that engaged peoples of color may encounter explicit or overt racism, or even the intimation of threat, as whites give voice to and thresh out the force of racism in their lives as raced subjects. We may fear creating or participating in the creation of another sort of silencing in which peoples of color will hear resonances of their past experiences of racism in the articulations of resistance and outrage by whites. Jay Sloan, the director of the writing center at Kent State University, wrote of a similar silencing effect during a recent dialogue about homophobia on the wcenter listserv. "I've certainly been guilty of falling silent," Jay wrote, "more than once when some external threat has reactivated the still potent personal fears that surround my own youth growing up as a gay man deeply closeted in a hostile social world." "But," Jay continued, "the fears that stymie vital conversations about difference in our universities are also deeply and resolutely political and institutional."[11]

Nuancing, by design, helps us and those whom we seek to teach or organize to understand the relationships between the articulations of threat, the fears those threats stimulate, and the political and institutional forces that promote and enforce silence. Studying the discursive practices that compose everyday racism can help all of us to be more conscious of when and how those practices are emerging in our dialogues with one another and in our writing to and for one another. But the reality is, I think, that there is no means or method by which we might address race matters without risking failures large and small. We simply will fail and so will our students. The true test of our

---

11. Jay Sloan to wcenter listserv, October 9, 2010, http://lists.uwosh.edu/mailman/listinfo/wcenter.

teaching and of student learning is the degree to which we are able to come unstuck from our failures and learn from them in reflective and deliberative ways, together.

Some significant element of the work of antiracism is to be a student, a researcher of failure. Probyn writes that "the researcher has to be open, even porous, to the rules, the dispositions, and the actions that constitute social life" (2005, 51). This is not to say, however, that the researcher need not engage critically with those rules, dispositions, and actions. In fact, this critical engagement is precisely the intellectual work of antiracism. When the voices of vigilance speak to us as we lead, organize, and teach—when anger, outrage, resistance, humiliation, silencing, or claims of blaming surface—our first impulse, individually and collectively, may be to foreclose dialogue. But there are other choices available to us.

These are moments when we might *sloooow* down, pause even, but stay with one another as we do; begin again to decenter, and then, with care, dig in. What forces or dynamics have set us quivering before one another? we might ask. What needs, interests, desires for relationship and for recognition drive our senses of having been shaken? How does what is happening or seems to have happened in this moment connect with other moments in our lived experience of being raced bodies/raced subjects? What seem to be the organizing concepts or representations of us as raced bodies/raced subjects at work on or over us in this moment? What are the social histories or genealogies of such concepts or representations? In what ways do these concepts or representations accrue meaning and significance within dominant and resisting racial ideologies? In what ways do these concepts or representations, or our resistance to them, connect to what passes for a prevailing "common sense" within a racially informed social order? These are the kinds of questions that attend the practices of nuancing.

From a rhetorical perspective, nuancing does not altogether abandon argumentation or persuasion traditionally conceived. But implicit in nuancing rhetoric is a recognition of the degree to which all argument, all persuasive writing and speech, bears within itself opacities of meaning and significance—references to prereason, to unnamed and unacknowledged prior or underlying "competences," to "irrationalities" (Crosswhite 1996, 189–190). Rather than dismissing the significance of these opacities, nuancing takes them in as part of or integral to its subject. Rhetors practicing nuancing essay among and between modes in order both to expose the existence of those opacities and to explore their dimensions. Finally, nuancing—understood as processual and recursive rhetorical practice—turns and re-turns to the questions that provoke the attempt, the essay, to begin with (199). In this sense, nuancing is provocative and transgressive: it engages critically with critique itself, successively questioning the questions with which critique engages (199). Like decentering, then, nuancing might be most successful to the extent that the text exceeds itself, to the extent that text fails "to achieve self-identity" or to be enough in and of itself (Butler 2005, 42).

Earlier in this chapter I wrote that nuancing is a form of antiracist action that also works to create conditions of possibility for action. James Crosswhite points out that traditional argument, misapplied, defers certain kinds of action. As an example he cites those moments in which we might be inclined to wrap our arms around one another in expression of comfort and care. "One part of cultural competence," he writes, "is knowing how to take actions of this sort immediately, without having to think of arguments for putting one's arm around another person . . . if we had to defend the action of putting our arms around other people to comfort them, it would tend to undermine the action of giving comfort immediately" (1996, 194). Nuancing, like traditional argument, I want to suggest, is not a substitute for the immediacies presented to us by the fact of our humanity. Nor is nuancing a means of crisis management. There are times when slumbering or silent racisms awaken or erupt and we are called to attend right here, right now, to the right here, right now. Nuancing, as a learned intellectual and affective discipline, does, I think, provide us with means by which to make generative strategic and tactical decisions about when and how to confront the exigencies of the most vicious and pernicious eruptions of racism. In or for these moments, nuancing is preparative; it is not, however, a prescription or an antidote.

At some level, nuancing begins with story: with what has happened to us or what has shaped our being, our perspectival and interpretive horizons, or with what happened merely a moment ago. Nuancing gives voice to memory, engages with, investigates, extends, and extrapolates from our individual and collective pasts. Nuancing stretches us across story, history, theory, across modes in search and re-search for understanding. The work of antiracism, though, calls us also to attend to the future—to possibilities of change agency in service of alternative ways of being, thinking, and doing in service of extending and expanding racial justice. We need to be willing and able to pursue the logics and moralities of racialization and racism into the future. We need to be willing and able to essay the barely imaginable: futures in which what race and the representations of raced bodies/raced subjects means—how race signifies within social organizations, systems, and institutions—is transformed.

We need means of pursuing the future perfect (the question of what we will have done or become), of composing ourselves and the world in service of alternative possibilities. In moving toward the future, to the extent that we leave the principles and practices of decentering and nuancing behind, we run the risk of reinventing that which we have already seen, felt, and come to know. But if we are able to carry these principles and practices forward, we may be able to conceive and compose toward more significant and more meaningful agency, more performative labors in service of racial justice, and in service of as yet unknown futures.

5

AN OPEN DOOR FOR ELIJAH

In the fall of 2009, the Midwest Writing Centers Association held its annual conference in Rapid City, South Dakota. I chose to drive to the meeting rather than fly, and I chose to drive alone rather than traveling with consultants from the UNL Writing Center who were taking a school van. I wanted to see more of Nebraska than would be available to me from the window of an airplane or from a van window as it hurtled along the interstate. I wanted to drive through the Rosebud Reservation in South Dakota, about which I had read a great deal. And I wanted to drive home through Pine Ridge to Wounded Knee, to stop there, and feel, somehow, that place and its history.

But there is another truth about my desire to drive to the conference. I love the experience of driving alone for long distances. I love casting myself into a journey. When I travel like this, I welcome the sense of being unmoored from the familiar. For me, the long road, the whoosh of wind over the car, the hum of wheels rolling over tarmac, take on a meditative quality. I lose for a time my sense of obligation to be myself as others know me, my sense of necessity to know my place in an ordered world, and to know where others belong in that world as well. The journey is an interstitial space and time between the known and the unknown. I am myself yet not myself. I know myself, yet am a stranger. I know the world yet the world is strange to me. I am drunk with the release from certainty—my consciousness of myself and others in the world shifting and transforming, opening with the landscapes through which I find my way.

In the opening pages of her book *A Field Guide to Getting Lost*, Rebecca Solnit describes the first time she got drunk. She was eight years old. At a Passover dinner, she mistook the goblet of wine set out for the prophet Elijah for her own glass and drank it down. Tradition holds, she writes, that Elijah will "come back to earth at the end of time and answer all the unanswerable questions" or "wander the earth in rags, answering difficult questions for scholars" (2005, 4). Passover tradition also includes leaving a door ajar so that when the prophet returns he will find an opening, a threshold between God's time and ours.

Solnit writes of the kind of altered consciousness (a kind of metaphorical drunkenness, at least in the sense of experiencing disequilibrium)—dislocated from the known, the familiar, and the certain—that might make us available intellectually, creatively, and spiritually to the possibility of learning that which we do not know at all. For Solnit, the most significant questions we can ask center around the unknown. How can we, she ponders, leave the door ajar for the unknown, "recognizing the role of the unforeseen . . . keeping your balance amid surprises . . . collaborating with chance . . . recognizing that there are some essential mysteries in the world and thereby a limit to calculation, to plan, to control. . . . To calculate on the unforeseen is perhaps exactly the paradoxical operation that life most requires of us" (2005, 5–6).

Social justice movements, generally, and antiracism is no exception, demand this kind of calculation. Those of us who seek transformative change are called to imagine worlds not yet seen—wrestling with the winds of history and present tenses that threaten always to foreclose such openings—to keep the door ajar for possibilities that inhere to the unknown and to futures that are inconceivable given what we think we know. There is a certain romanticism, perhaps—a certain appealing mystery—to imagining the unknown as possibility and enacting an "open stance," as Ratcliffe might say, to uncertainty (2006, 26). But there is this as well: the open door at Passover is an expression of trust in God's protection against persecution and oppression. The tradition, some say, began during the Middle Ages with the practice of blood libel: the accusation by Christians—that Jews made a practice of killing Christian babies and drinking their blood—as a justification for persecution and oppression. An open door meant both that Jews celebrating Passover could watch out for Christians intent on blood libel, or, according to others, that Christians could peer in and see for themselves that wine, not blood, filled the goblets of worshippers (Passover 2003).[1] We ignore histories of domination and the material conditions of oppression in the present at our peril. An open door is a risk. The opening, the joint, the articulation between peoples is as dangerous and fragile a place as it is a locus of possibility.

Those of us who have been raced white may seek the doorframe, the space in-between, the open stance, from that place turn our gaze toward the Other and, speaking or representing from that joint, craft a stance of rhetorical innocence (not openness at all), claiming a transcendence of or absolution from whiteliness that we have not earned and that is not, in fact, possible. We may perform from that place that form of whiteliness Scott Lyons terms "rhetorical imperialism: the ability of dominant powers to assert control of others by setting the terms of debate. These terms are often definitional—that is, they identify the parties discussed by describing them in certain ways" (2000, 452). And we might perform from that place that Gerald Vizenor critiques as "manifest manners": representing into presence or attempting to make manifest that which is absent, the imaginary Other—often infused with nostalgia and/or the logics of Manifest Destiny—the simulation that distorts the real and so claims or reclaims authority over and against that which is or more likely might be (1994, see especially 39–44).

My point is not that we ought not narrate or interrogate our lives from this place, but that, left undisturbed, habitual and learned epistemologies and rhetorics of whiteliness will

---

1. Michelle Jones, Opening the door for Elijah, *On a Path* (blog), January 13, 2011, http://michellejones.net/onapath/2011/01/elijah.php.

reproduce the conditions for their own emergence and reproduction. They will sustain, whatever our intentions, the material
conditions that attend racial oppression, however absurd the
idea of race may be on its face. We need another point of view,
a way of conceiving, thinking, representing (ourselves) that is
simultaneously open and resisting, transgressive of racial logics
and the rules of racial standing, and oppositional to them: fragile, tentative, yielding, and even so animated by that life force
that refuses finitudes.

Ask nearly anyone who has driven across Nebraska about
the state and you will hear "flat and boring." Full stop. It is true
that if you drive west through the state along Interstate 80, you
are, in fact, in for several hours of flat prairie land that, from
a car at least, seems unending in its monotony. But my route
to the MWCA conference took me north from Grand Island,
away from the interstate, through the Sand Hills that rise up
from the Ogallala Aquifer. The landscape changes slowly, nearly
imperceptibly, from that imperturbable prairie to rolling hills
covered with low grasses and brush. As I entered the Sand
Hills region, I imagined I had suddenly encountered a desert
until I realized I was also passing shallow lakes curling around
the feet of the hills. The Sand Hills of Nebraska are, in fact, a
large, complex, and delicate system of wetlands—the largest in
the United States. This is a liminal place, I realized—a space
in-between—and, as is the way of wetlands, the ecosystems that
border the Sand Hills depend upon its existence. The wetlands
are the joint, the hinge between incompatible places. They are
the condition of possibility for relations between ecosystems
that otherwise might encroach upon, damage, perhaps destroy
one another.

What would it mean, I wondered to myself as I drove
through the Sand Hills, to think like a wetland? In an essay
penned decades ago, writer and environmentalist Aldo Leopold
describes the day he killed a wolf and learned, he says, to think
like a mountain. An avid deer hunter, Leopold had seen the
wolf as a threat to the plenitude of deer available to hunt. When

he and his hunting companions encounter a wolf and her cubs, they don't even consider the possibility of not shooting them, but fire furiously into the pack. The mother wolf receives a killing shot and Leopold describes watching her die there on a mountainside. He writes,

> We reached the old wolf in time to watch a fierce green fire dying in her eyes. I realized then, and have known ever since, that there was something new to me in those eyes—something known only to her and to the mountain. I was young then, and full of trigger-itch; I thought that because fewer wolves meant more deer, that no wolves would mean hunters' paradise. But after seeing the green fire die, I sensed that neither the wolf nor the mountain agreed with such a view. (n.d.)

Leopold learns from the dying wolf the lesson that decisions informed by convictions about one's right to dominate, in service of that domination, and agitated by a sense of immediacy and certain valuations of efficiency and expediency, may leave a world diminished, even decimated, for those who come after. Leopold learns, he writes, to hear in the howl of the wolf not a threat to one's desires, but a call to attend to the consciousness of the mountain, to conceive of time and all that matters as the matter of deep time and big history.

A mountain seems immoveable. While day and night, light and shadow, and shifting seasons may sweep across its face, a mountain remains: obdurate. To think like a wetland is also to think and to matter in deep time. The wetland seems to submit or yield to the floods, to the effluvium of its borderlands, even as it goes to work sifting the detritus, absorbing and transforming in service of life that thrives on the in-between. To think like this, like wetlands, I imagine, one must create and recreate endlessly a sense of self that emerges not from the self/other binary (I am not you nor are you me), but rather from one's relations. To absorb and transform the aftermath of the flood that has passed even as the next flood rises, to make sense of that which remains over and over again, is the labor of a life understood as extending far beyond the lifespan of one human—not bounded by her birth and death but as the labor of one who is of and for the many: those who come before and those who will come after. To think in this way, I reflected, and consequently to be in the world in this way, is to recognize that one's actions, one's work in the world, and one's acceptance of the flood as a condition of one's being, makes and remakes our relations over endless time endlessly.

In his book *Time and the Art of Living*, Robert Grudin writes of a general tendency among scholars and writers to "view the past mechanistically [in terms of cause and effect] and the future teleologically [in terms of goal or purpose]" (1997, 62). We tend, in other words, "to forget past purposes and to ignore future causes." And this tendency, Grudin notes, "results in faulty analyses and mistaken predictions, in a loss of moral consistency, in a failure to use memory as an effective guide to planning and, above all, in an alienation from the reality of time as a continuum" (62). To conceive of the world, to think and to write in this way, is to assert mere certainty and so constrain the vitality and changeability of one's relations. To conceive, to think, and to write in this way is to extend rather than contend with the complexity of race and racism.

As I was doing research for this chapter, thrashing around for words to name the concepts that would provide its anchor, I came across an essay by artist and musician Brian Eno. In it, Eno tells a story about having been invited by a wealthy friend to a party shortly after he moved to New York City. He describes taking a taxi to his friend's home, and as the cab travels through increasingly poor and apparently dangerous neighborhoods, he begins to worry that he has gotten the wrong address or that the cab driver has misunderstood where he wants to go. He arrives at a huge old warehouse on a nearly deserted street inhabited only by a few old drunken men, rings the bell, and is buzzed into the dusty old building by his friend. When he arrives, by freight elevator, at her apartment on an upper floor, the world in which he finds himself is utterly transformed. Here is a glittering, dazzling display of wealth. He steps out of the elevator into what he describes as "a multi-million dollar palace." "The contrast with the rest of the building and the street outside," he writes, "couldn't have been starker." As the evening wore on, Eno says, he talked with his hostess. "'Do you like it here?' I asked. 'It's the best place I've ever lived', she replied. 'But I mean, you know, is it an interesting neighbourhood?' 'Oh—the neighbourhood? Well . . . that's outside!' she laughed." (2001)

Eno describes the apparent mindscape of his hostess as fitting within a social and cultural pattern of perception and thought he terms "'The Small Here'": a kind of crabbed and shrunken conception of the world in which what matters is only the space immediately before us or which we occupy—in and through which we move right here, right now. Eno finds a parallel to this radically localized conception of space in a social and cultural perception of time he terms "'The Short Now,'" in which lives are focused nearly exclusively on that which is immediate, rapid, dynamic, and "lively," but are also lived on "selfish, irresponsibly, and randomly dangerous" terms. In his essay, Eno urges readers to reach for a radically more expansive sense of space and time: a *big* here and a *l...o...n...g* now. He advocates for a world-view that acknowledges the interconnectedness of multiple spaces and long-time pasts and futures in service of reaching for "a frame of mind where it comes to seem unacceptable—gauche, uncivilized—to act in disregard of our descendants." Eno writes, "'Now' is never just a moment. The Long Now is the recognition that the precise moment you're in grows out of the past and is a seed for the future. The longer your sense of Now, the more past and future it includes" (2001).

Search on Wikipedia for *deep time* and you will find this line in the entry: "An understanding of geologic history and the concomitant history of life requires a comprehension of time which initially may be disconcerting."[2] I laugh when I read it. "Disconcerting." The line makes irony of understatement. To

---

2. See http://en.wikipedia.org/wiki/Deep_time.

imagining making and remaking one's relations in the big here and the long now is to think vertiginously, to cast one's habituated sense of self-as-I backward into the abyss of history and forward into vast expanses of time-yet-to-come. Still more, to imagine in this way is to extend and multiply one's sense of accountability and to whom one might be accountable or to whom one might be called to offer an account of oneself in ways that are catastrophic to rectitude, to knowability, to certainty. *I* is unmappable here; there is no north to compass, or every direction is all directions. To think in this way is to lose one's way.

Night was falling as I wound my way across the Rosebud Reservation, watching for turns, missing them, backtracking to right my course. I stopped for gas, coffee, and directions at a convenience store where teenagers huddled, gossiping and laughing. I smiled at them and they laughed some more. They are mocking me, I thought, and felt a spurt of resentment. Me! Come to bear witness! "What do you send me a message like that for?. . . How am I a hog and me both? How am I saved and from hell too" (O'Connor 1992, 507). I recognized and was surprised by that Mrs. Turpin in me and I laughed too. "The nature of survivance," writes Vizenor, "creates a sense of narrative resistance to absence, literary tragedy, nihility, and victimry" (2009, 35–38). The mock, the tease, is a rhetorical move of survivance. To justify one's simulation of presence in such a moment—the moment of the mock—is so often to manifest the ways in which one's "presence" is a fake. To justify is to simulate a self that is not and cannot be as well as an Other that is so much more the specter of one's own morose nostalgia for a time that never was than a presence whom one might address, to whom one might appeal for direction or guidance.

"Stories," writes Malea Powell citing Vizenor, "have the power to make, remake, unmake the world" (2002, 396). Survivance—survival and resistance—stories, she notes, "reimagine and, literally, refigure 'the Indian.'" A survivance story "transforms . . . object-status within colonial discourse into a subject-status, a presence instead of an absence" (400). The survivance story is neither the story nor the work of those of us who have been raced white. This much we have in common, perhaps, with the imaginary Indian of paracolonial discourse: raced white is also an imaginary (Powell, 399; Vizenor 1993, 77). Those of us who have been raced white need not trouble, trick, or mock paracolonial discourse, however, in order to achieve subject-status. The acquiescent (or consensually hallucinating) white already possesses the means to realize that achievement in whiteliness. The work of antiracism is not to reimagine and refigure white. Yielding—succumbing and resisting by allying with resistance—is our work; the telling of stories, casting of narratives that undermine, that subvert, that defigure white as a present-absence, that evacuate the *I* that presupposes an Other, is our work. We might also have to learn to live with the reality that those for whom survivance stories are the way may need or choose to maintain the fact of a doorway—that signifier of difference—that can yet close. We might also, then, resist the vacuous identifications with Other that seek to elide histories of oppression, of genocide, of the remarkable evil the idea of white has done and still does in the world. We, too, should mock the idea of white and, even as we love humanity, seek the death of that idea.

I drove on from that place, smiling to myself, finally, about teenagers who know the world well enough to laugh at an old white lady in the chill of an autumn evening. It isn't wrong to smile in such moments, I hope. But it is or should be hard to pass through such a place and time, and through the momentary relation made by mockery, without being troubled also. Look, the poverty on Rosebud is unmistakable—in the crumbling infrastructure of roads and public buildings; the houses that seem barely able to stand let alone withstand the winter winds that must buffet them when the cold comes on and settles in to stay; in the thinness of dogs that race passing cars, barking wildly. However tempting it may be to deny one's agency in the establishment and maintenance of such conditions, this is the question to which we must be called. I wondered as I passed through how I might make sense of, how I might understand the historical sweep of violence, of pain, of loss, of poverty over and through peoples of such faith without conflating those forces and without reducing, somehow, that people's faith to an effect and, hence, a justification and legitimation of suffering—to an easy, slippery explanation of survival and consequent occlusion of resistance, excusing us, excusing me, from responsibility not only for the past, but for the future: from accountability in deep time.

Darkness fell as I slipped my car into a line of traffic heading west across I-90. In time, I grew tired and needed to rest and stretch. I pulled off into a roadside rest stop and stepped from the car. The air was chilly and I shivered a little as I zipped up my jacket. Wandering a bit away from the streetlights illuminating the parking lots and sidewalks, I stepped onto the grass, walked a short way, and nearly ran into a sign. I looked up, making out its message dimly through the gloom: "Beware of Rattlesnakes." Slowly and ridiculously, I backed away, returning to safety of more established paths. I followed the sidewalk back to my car.

There are always a few warning signs at the borders of the small-here. They tell us to be wary, but what they really mean is *stop*. Beyond this point lies the serpent, waiting. There is risk beyond the sign that marks the borders of the known. But there are ways of moving through risk. Warning signs don't offer instructions in how to move; that's not their job. They tell you to stop moving. Try starting a dialogue about racism in predominantly, traditionally, or habitually whitely company and I guarantee you someone will post the warning sign. *Stop*. The sign demarcates the safety of the known. Where we are, this place we occupy, we own, in and over which we prevail, is the place where we ought to be, the sign implies. That place beyond the certainty and rightness of where we are, is where we ought not, need not go. The sign will not say, nor will the one who posts the sign say, that whatever the risks beyond the line of demarcation between the known and the unknown, danger is already inside the bounds, inside me, inside you. The biggest risks in stepping past the sign are (a) that you are likely to get lost and must contend therefore with not knowing and (b) that you will carry danger within you into the unknown and discover as you move that, at least some of the time, you are as the snake. You will have to contend with that as well.

Arrivals are always difficult for me. Having traveled in journey consciousness—dislocated from any felt obligation to know myself, to be myself, to think and feel in ways others might expect of me or find intelligible—to arrive is to relocate as one who is known and knowable. After hundreds of miles and hours of silence, arriving necessitates speaking and even that is hard for me. I have to work at it. In time, however, I come back to myself. At conferences—particularly those I attend regularly—I have a regular crew of friends with whom I attend sessions and share meals. One evening at the MWCA conference, I went out for dinner with some of these folks. We chose a nice Italian restaurant in downtown Rapid City that offered excellent wine, service, and food: a place for the well-heeled. Between courses, my best friend and I went outside to smoke, seating ourselves in the chilly night on a bench on the street.

An Indian girl and boy came toward us down the sidewalk. Some distance behind them walked two men, the hoods of their coats pulled up over their heads so that their faces were hidden. The girl stopped when she reached us and sat on the bench beside me; the boy remained standing, hands in his pockets, shifting uneasily on his feet. I could feel her trembling. She asked me for a cigarette and I gave her one. "Those men," she breathed, "they're following us. They want me to go with them." Her hand shook as she lifted the cigarette to her lips. "This is my cousin," she said, indicating the boy, who stood listening, waiting. "He is too young to fight." They were both young; too young, I thought, to be on the cold streets of Rapid City on such a night. The men watched us from a distance. They walked out of sight and then back again to stand on the corner. My friend, who seems fearless to me, stood, faced them, and put her hands on her hips. She stood there staring at them, her cigarette dangling from her lips, until they moved out of sight again. We asked the girl and boy if they had a safe place to go and the girl said they had an apartment, if only they could get there. "Go," we told them. "Go. We'll watch for you. We stood there on the sidewalk in the cold and watched them until they were out of sight. Then we went back inside the restaurant, rejoined our companions, drank our wine and ate our meals.

And through the clink of tableware, the laughter, and the chatter, I worried. And remembered teenagers laughing, mocking. Relations are made. History accretes. Survivance counters the violence of racism and the victimry racism produces in its targets; survivance counters the death of hope. But there are places and times in the right-here, right-now, by God, when the brutality of the conditions produced by racial domination and white supremacy are undeniable. Places and times when one's own complicity snakes out of hiding and turns, hissing, to bite you on the ass.

I should have gone to get the car and driven those kids to their apartment instead of returning to eat and drink in the safety of the restaurant. I should at least have walked some way with them. I felt the prickle of fear in my gut. What if those men had come after me too? I should have brought those kids in here, asked the waiter to make room for them at the table. I should have fed them and tried to learn where their parents are, who's responsible for them; I should have tried to get them help. I thought about the limit on my credit card, which I was already dangerously close to overreaching. I thought about the ways that, even given what I had seen, I could not presume to know the histories of those kids or anything about their current circumstances other than that in the moment of our encounter they had been in trouble. I knew I had not done enough. I could not conceive of what might constitute enough. As we made our way back to the hotel, I peered in every direction looking for the kids and the men who stalked them. The streets of Rapid City were empty and still.

Epic failure. There are some moments for which we cannot be ready. There are some moments in which our readiness, such as it is, may fail us. Our self-interest, our self-centeredness, the fear such moments provoke that freezes us or tunnels our vision impede not only our ability to act, but also our ability to conceive of how we might act. Here's a hard reality: in the small-here and the short-now such moments matter terribly and tragically. In a big-here and a long-now, these moments and the failures they represent matter more for the possibility of survivance actualized; they matter for the possibility that we—those who fail and those who survive and resist such failures—might learn to make and matter our relations differently. While we cannot change the fact of failure or the effects of failure on others in such moments, we do in fact have agency when it comes to our own learning. We can choose to hide the truth, to pretend as if that thing that just happened never happened. We can choose to blame our failures on others or on histories from which we absolve ourselves of responsibility. Or we can choose to lean in, to stay with the possibility of learning, which is not to say that we may ever come to fully understand or to certainty. We can stay with and in the flood and its messes, sifting, processing, decomposing, and turning them slowly, slowly, slowly into the conditions that make living in a big here and a long now—in deep time—possible. We can stay with learning, understanding that slow doesn't mean no learning, understanding that there are moments when slow is inadequate, but slow is all there is when what we are learning is how to think, how to speak, how to write a discourse we are making as we move.

I left the conference early on the final day in order to arrive at Wounded Knee well before sunset. I drove southeast under a lowering sky, skirting the outer edges of the Badlands. By the time I reached the Pine Ridge Reservation, rain had overtaken me and I drove for some time along a winding way, through small towns and across the long distances between them, as the water ran in rivulets down the windshield of my car, the wipers struggling to keep up. The rain stopped. And started. And the clouds lay low over the hills and gullies. When I arrived at the site of the massacre, I parked in a muddy lot below the Wounded Knee Memorial and waited for a shower to pass. When the rain had ceased once more, I walked up the hill toward the cemetery, opened the little gate, and entered. I knelt, then, and prayed. And wept. There is too much to mourn in this world and no language that speaks sorrow in all its depth and dimension, just as there is no language that speaks utter joy. These are feelings or sensations so abundant, so excessive, they manifest beyond the reach of reason, of rationality. They cannot be spoken.

There is something obscene in the gesture of the raced-white, whitely woman, sister of a stolen child, praying in such a place. And yet there are places in this world and memories and histories and ghosts who will bring just such a one to her knees. I try for words. I do not want to speak with God, I want to speak with history; I want to converse with the dead, as if those murdered in that place might tell me where and how to find the in-between. The winds mock me. I don't need forgiveness and I don't need absolution. I am searching for the commodious language of ghosts and griots. Searching for the excessive language of lovers and the transgressive language of holy fools. Searching for the language of radicals and revolutionaries: the language that refuses—that cries out *no* and means it—even as it opens itself to the unbearable, unimaginable *yes* of alliance and so on to hope.

I do not know how long I knelt there. When I raised my head and looked about me, three men stood at the gate, their horses tethered to the cemetery fence. One was older than the others and stood before them, waiting for me, silent and watchful. One stood close by the horses. One stood in-between, wearing an AIM sweatshirt. All three held dream catchers, little leather pouches, and beaded necklaces in their hands. They had come to sell me these things and recognized in me, perhaps, one who likes a story. I listened as they described what their parents and grandparents had said of the occupation at Wounded Knee in

1973. They described the flight of an airplane, low over the village, evading the FBI's blockade and Dick Wilson's checkpoints to drop packages of food for the people.

I petted their horses and they told me of the annual ride taken each December to honor Chief Big Foot and his people who were murdered at Wounded Knee. The ride, they said, follows the route Big Foot and his people took in flight from the 7th Cavalry, beginning in North Dakota at the gravesite of Sitting Bull and culminating at the site of the massacre at Wounded Knee. One of their horses, they said, had made the trek. The others would go this year, in December. They described the cold, the bitter wind against which horses and riders struggle on the way, the hardness of the journey, the lack of food, and also the joy, the celebration, the honor of the way. I bought a trinket from each of them, one for each of my children, and turned away to return to the graveyard. The men mounted their horses and cantered away down the hill.

I knelt again. And it rained again.

When I rose once more and looked down toward the road by which I had come to this place, I saw that an old man and an old woman stood beside my car, waiting. I walked out of the cemetery, closing the gate behind me. When I reached them, the woman grumbled, "We've told those boys to wait down here to sell their stuff, not to disturb you up there. We all agreed that's what we would do." She motioned to me to follow her to a kiosk where she had laid out jewelry and also a binder overflowing with newspaper clippings and other papers. "Listen," she said. And she began to tell stories. "There," and she gestured toward the banks of a creek, "is where the massacre happened." "That way," and she gestured again, "is where the people came from." And she described the massacre, the demand that the warriors give up their weapons, their reluctance, the firing of a single shot, and then the blast of fire from four Hotchkiss guns alongside the rifle fire that ripped into the bodies of men, women, and babies without regard for age or innocence. For three days, as a blizzard raged, the bodies of the dead lay on the banks of Wounded Knee Creek before the army had them buried. Twenty Medals of Honor were awarded to soldiers from the 7th Cavalry who participated in the massacre or in the roundup of the survivors—more medals of honor than for any other battle fought by the U.S. government anywhere, at any time in history.

The old woman paged through her binder, pointing at yellowed clippings and faded pages of manuscript. "Not so long ago," she told me, "the government came along and offered to clean up this place and make it nice, so people would come here like they go to Mount Rushmore." I looked up and around me. The sign announcing that this is the site of the massacre at Wounded Knee is old and faded and covered with graffiti; the fence that surrounds the cemetery is bent and rusted. Weeds grow up among the stones in the graveyard. The place is both beautiful and unkempt. It surely doesn't look like a national historic monument. I smiled at her and imagined the hint of a tease. "Our elders met and talked," she says. "They thanked the government for its kind offer and said we would be happy to accept if they would take back those twenty Medals of Honor and apologize for what the 7th Cavalry did on that day. The government went away and they have not come back." I look at her. I look at the binder. I look at the old man who is gazing away at some point I cannot perceive. I'm not crying now. Tears would be an insult, I think, to a story that shakes with laughter and with rage. The story of the trick that exposes the emptiness of the gesture—to create a place where hundreds, thousands maybe, will come to kneel, to remember, and to honor without ever answering the question of who is to be honored.

"Not all the people died, you know," she says to me. I turn to her once more. "No, not everyone died." There would be silence, but for the wind. "Yes, some were able to crawl away into the gullies and underbrush and hide. And some babies were wrapped in blankets and protected from the cold by their mothers' bodies where they fell. Some of the babies lived." And then she told me this story:

"One of the babies who lived was a little girl. This little girl, Lost Bird, was taken by an officer who came after the massacre. His name was General Colby. Anyway, he took this little baby who lived home with him to Nebraska, where you come from," and she jerked her head at the license plate on my car. "To a town called Beatrice. And gave the baby to his wife to raise up as their own. They adopted this baby. His wife was for women's rights; she was a suffragette, but I guess she didn't think too much about the Indians. She tried to raise Lost Bird up white. The people in that family abused that little child. They hurt her bad. One day, the general left his wife and Lost Bird and wouldn't support them, wouldn't give them any money anymore. Lost Bird grew up to be a woman. She tried to come home to her people, but we couldn't recognize her. She was too different from us after all those years. We didn't treat her so good. And so she left again and lived in California for a while. Maybe she sold herself to get by. After a while Lost Bird died and she was buried in California. But the people here didn't forget her. The people felt badly about how Lost Bird was treated when she tried to come home. Finally, back in 1990 or '91 maybe, we brought her here to be with her people again. She's up there now," and she gestured to the hilltop cemetery, "with her people again." Later I learned that an organization had been formed in honor of Lost Bird, the Lost Bird Society, to assist in reuniting Indian children taken from their homes for adoption in white families with their tribes.

How did you know, I wanted to howl, to tell that story to me? How did you know about Rick? Oh, I wanted then to make of her a witch, a shaman, a healer—mender of that which is broken in me. But maybe she was saying that I really didn't have to come to this place to rubberneck at racism. Could have stayed in my own state. Could have stayed in my own home, truth be told. Could come back when those twenty Medals of Honor have been rescinded. When apologies have been made. And restitution. And the Black Hills returned to their peoples.

But I had lost my words. So I asked her a question I had also posed to the young men on the hill. "Don't you ever get tired of telling these stories to white people who don't know the history? To tourists?" I am pretending I am not a tourist, among other things. Her answer, despite the generational difference between her and the young men and the differences between the stories they chose to tell, was the same. "This is what I am here to do. This is how we remember and this is how we honor our ancestors. We tell the story. This is our job."

I imagine a labor passed on from generation to generation, learned at the breast or the knee or in the intimacy of moments like these at least. And maybe there is this trace, or crease, as Vizenor might say, in the work. And there is this as well: the jewelry, the dream catchers, the hand-sewn and beaded leather pouches, are laid out there for purchase; the stories create obligation. She is not selling victimry, but making a mockery of it. Selling survivance to one who may or may not recognize that which she has purchased. She stories at the hinge, the coordinating conjunction—and apparently contradictory possibilities can be simultaneously realized.

I left the reservation with the gathering of evening, making my way back along the rim of the high plains down into the Sand Hills and then onto the prairies, the words of the old woman ringing in my ears, abiding with me. "This is our job."

Pragmatic antiracism is work; it is on-the-ground activism. The productiveness of antiracist activism in a big here and a long now depends upon our willingness and our ability to excavate and articulate the racial histories of the systems, institutions, and communities that structure our lived experience as raced beings. The on-the-ground work of antiracism is to expose and examine the roles those systems, institutions, and communities play within and in service of the logics of race, the rules of racial order, and the perpetuation of white supremacy; you need to learn how to do this. Carefully, analytically, incisively, you need to learn to notice, be troubled by, name, and contend with the principles, philosophies, and theories espoused by systems and institutions (and the individuals who labor within them) and the principles, philosophies, and theories actually in use within those webs or sites (Barr and Tagg 2003 2–3). In other words, you need to learn to name and critique the disparities and contradictions between what systems and institutions say they stand for and what and how they actually do what they do.

To do the pragmatic work of antiracism, you also need to learn how to organize and strategize. You need to learn how to look for the weak link in a system or institution—and by weak I mean not the most racist person or institutional site, but the person or site most ready for yielding, amenable to change, most willing to withdraw consent and cooperation. You need to be able to plan and to build consensus around goals and priorities for change. Networking is a good skill to have for the job of antiracism; imperative to this work is the will and ability to create and sustain connections across and throughout a system or an institution. It helps to know the rules, spoken (like Robert's Rules of Order) and unspoken (like what *not* to act like if you want to get tenure or promotion or just plain keep your job). This helps because there are ways to speak and write that sound like you're down with the rules, when really what you're doing is changing them or subverting them. It helps to know the rules so you can bend and break them strategically when possible and as an act of refusal when necessary. It helps to know how to move minds, creating a critical tilt toward change.

Intercultural diversity trainer Patricia Digh writes that racism is a "wicked problem." Tame problems, she writes, have "a well-defined and stable problem statement; a definite stopping point; a solution that can be objectively evaluated as being right or wrong; solutions that can be tried and abandoned; and belongs to a class of similar problems that can be solved in a similar manner" (2007). In contrast, wicked problems, notes Digh, are hard to define. Wicked problems tap into strongly held religious, political, economic, and professional positions and convictions such that finding consensus around possible solutions is extremely difficult. Further, Digh writes, wicked problems don't hold still; they are fluid "sets of complex, interacting issues evolving in a dynamic social context." She goes on to say that "often, new forms of wicked problems emerge *as a result* of trying to understand and solve one of them. While attempting to solve a wicked problem, the solution of one of its aspects may reveal or create another, even more complex problem; like a Rubik's cube, solving one facet changes the face of other sides" (italics in original). Further, Digh notes, even when we acknowledge that racism is a wicked problem, very often the solutions we propose, the interventions we invent, are tame. And the application of tame solutions to wicked problems, Digh writes, makes wicked problems worse, not better—makes wicked problems multiply, twist and morph, setting off streams of other related wicked problems.

Beware of the warning sign. The wickedness of the problem of racism provides an opportunity, perhaps even an invitation, for gatekeepers at the open door to claim that there is nothing to be done and that to do anything is to make everything worse. Antiracist activists assert that as wicked a problem as racism may be, it is a problem that possesses rhetorical exigency—the problem is amenable to change or transformation through discourse. Antiracist activists invoke human agency. We say that the causes of or conditions for this exigency are related to choices made by human agents that those agents might also make other kinds of choices. Part of what makes racism a wicked problem is the occlusion of agency in public discourse about it. Racism accretes wickedness or apparently intractable complexity (inaccessibility to discourse) with each successive denial of agency and, hence, of power and ability to do something, anything, to address its exigency. Oh, racism vexes. It is intractable, no doubt. But the fact of its wickedness does not undo its rhetorical exigency.

Antiracist activist movements full-stop fail when tame thought and tame rhetorics—thought and rhetorics infused with unexamined, uncritiqued whiteliness—prevail within the coalition. Antiracist activist movements fail as individuals are tapped too often to step up to the sign that warns off all of us and marks as targets those individuals we elect as ones to be feared, avoided, isolated, and shamed. Individuals sent alone over and over again to the demarcation line grow tired, and begin to recognize in these endless elections the manifestations of whiteliness in simulations of antiracism. Antiracist activist movements fail not so much because systems, institutions, and the acquiescent within them deny the rhetorical exigency of racism. Rather, they fail when activists themselves, having never learned, really, how to create and sustain big-here/long-now multiracial alliances, begin to deny that exigency.

This is to say, the wild, vertiginous thinking and making of meaning that sustains rhetorical exigency within the domain of the wicked problem is both made possible and conditioned by the making of relations at the joint. "We need," as Malea Powell writes, "a language that allows us to imagine respectful and reciprocal relationships that acknowledge the degree to which we need one another (have needed one another) in order to survive and flourish" (2004, 41). We do not get to claim we possess those relations by fiat (at least not without being mocked). For those of us who are raced white, there is labor that attends both creating and sustaining this commodious language with and for those with whom we would make our relations; labor that is different from though interdependent with the survivance work that antiracist peoples of color do. Neither form of labor replaces on-the-ground activism, but together these labors make that activism possible and sustainable in a big here and a long now.

Philosophically, epistemologically, and pragmatically, antiracist theory and practice demand of all of us that we remember our own histories and that we bear witness to our lived experience as raced beings where witness is understood to be distinct from historiography—aimed less at the performance of objective and disinterested narration than at the offering of memories cast in stories designed to resist the absences, the silences, that attend forgetting what and whom has come before (Booth 2006, 73). We are called to testify to the materiality of the world racism has wrought, to our own lived experience and to the lived experiences of our relations in that world. And we call on others—those who might hear us, those who will listen—to recognize and acknowledge that past that we bear and that they may bear as well (72). To bear witness and to testify is also to demand, to press toward a different sort of present and future in the sense of calling either for a return or for a transformation.

One of the things I believe—and I think I learned to believe this in and through the antiracism movement—is that part of what makes all of us human is the way in which we humans tend to tell a story in order to understand a story. Sometimes we tell a story in order to understand the very story we are telling as we tell it; sometimes we tell a story in order to understand anOther story. We sift and make sense of the excess of our relations and the detritus floods of such excess leave in our lives, making and remaking our relations through narratives we offer across a wide array of rhetorical contexts, claiming our nearness as well as our distance from one another. We use stories to sort and slice away the past from the present as well as using them to connect the past with the now. We need not only to discern how to choose, given the various contexts in which we might speak and write of race and racism, between the mechanistic and the teleological; we need also and especially a rhetoric through which we might move fluidly among and between them: a rhetoric or rhetorics that might account for myriad ways of understanding, for coming to recognize and offer rich accounts of the composition of histories, present tenses, and future possibilities.

Critical race theorists have long used the practice of storytelling to trouble or destabilize claims to universality that continue to prevail in courts of law, in evaluations of the scholar and of scholarship, in political and economic discourses, within and across communities. Law professor and writer Patricia A. Williams writes that such universalist epistemologies and rhetorics are characterized by three critical features: (1) the treatment of abstractions as concrete realities or the "hypostatization" of the abstract in order to make complex conditions simple, (2) claims of universal, a priori truths, laws, or codes that seem to transcend historical moment and social context, and (3) "the existence of objective, 'unmediated' voices by which those transcendent, universal truths find their expression" (1992, 8–9). Williams notes that judges, lawyers, and legal theorists are frequently accorded such status. We might add scholars and teachers, politicians and community leaders, pundits and . . . until at some point we realize we are listing those who acquiesce to and enact whiteliness, who enact rhetorical imperialism, who etch their lives across logics of race and rules of racial standing, who are content to stand without, gatekeeping the open door, gazing in and ready to accuse.

Williams notes also that such voices exist and possess universality by virtue of the often implicit or coded legitimation of certain romanticized representations of the voices of "the people" packaged as stereotype: "the Noble Savage as well as the Great White Father, the Good-Hearted Masses, the Real American, the Rational Consumer" (1992, 9). Williams writes that "much of what is spoken in so-called objective, unmediated voices is in fact mired in hidden subjectivities and unexamined claims that make property of others beyond the self, all the while denying such connections." The use of such voices, Williams suggests, involves the activity of displacing one's subjectivity through the creation of an "authority who [is] imaginary, but whose rhetorical objectivity [is] as smooth and convincing as a slice of the knife" (11). And this authority can claim that it may legitimately represent the needs and desires of an imagined Other. This authority can, and frequently does, defeat authentic group interests through the (mindless) assertion of the primacy of individual experience and rights, through the practice of exceptionalism: finding one or a few individuals whose lives or experiences can be represented as countering the claims to experience of a group, and using that representation to call the expressed needs and desires of that group into question. This practice enables "recasting the general group experience as a fragmented series of specific isolated events rather than a pervasive social phenomenon (13).

These are the effects of whiteliness, and to the extent that they snake their way into antiracist activist movements, they poison the epistemological and rhetorical arts of antiracism (Powell 2004, 43). Vizenor writes that "we are sustained in stories, by the natural reason of our imagination, but the tragedy 'to go unimagined' has dominated most interpretations of tribal remembrance" (1993, 67). If those of us who are raced white are to join with peoples of color in the creation of the commodious thought and language of antiracism, we must learn to recognize and resist whiteliness working in and through *us* even as we share the work of antiracist activism with peoples of color.

The work of antiracism demands that we learn to do certain tasks, learn certain means of negotiating, advocating, agitating, and demanding change within a variety of institutional and systemic contexts. But we cannot do any of this, cannot do this at all, if we allow whitely ways of thinking to tame our languages and our rhetorics. We have to learn to break the codes of conduct whiteliness both imposes and enforces. We need to be disobedient, recalcitrant, diss-functional subjects when whiteliness is at the door. We need to spend less time superimposing our unimaginative simulations of Others over and against those with whom we would make relations and more time imagining ourselves as beings capable of wild love that exceeds and transgresses the multiple purposes and meanings of an open door for Elijah.

The point of antiracist epistemology and rhetoric is not to elevate the story, any story, or the "personal," to parallel or equivalent status with the universal, authoritative voice, but to unhinge that powerful voice from its claims to universality and authority. Nor is the point to *believe* uncritically the stories of individuals. The point is to lean into stories of survivance, to hear, see, feel the revelation of that which has been suppressed, to feel the wrinkles, the creases, the teases in the story, and to learn from them. The point is to reach for discernment of the ways in which the survivance stories of peoples of color, and the yielding stories antiracist whites labor to tell, are interconnected and interdependent upon one another; the point is to extend those stories beyond the individual into the historical experience of a group.

Significant to this book is the recognition that stories of the racial experiences of whites are also suppressed—albeit in different ways, for different purposes, and with different effects—to occlude the significance of racial identity to the lived experience, social standing, access, and privilege of whites. The challenge of antiracist epistemology and rhetoric for whites is to write into that suppressed story one's own commonality, but also agency, responsibility, and accountability: to explore the interrelationships between one's own story and that which has been suppressed, not as aberrational experience, but as either collective or contiguous historical, social, and lived experience. And the point is to diss-function whiteliness, writing one-as-relation into suppressed stories not as a means of conscription or appropriation, but through the sustained practice of transmemoration: of remembering without denying, suppressing, or stealing the memories of others.

There is work to be done in resistance to racism and there are ways to share the work. But how to be and become an ally is not self-evident. We who are raced white have to learn to unmake our selves in order that we might make allies of ourselves. We need to learn to imagine that we might not only see, but also be and become in and of the mind of deep time. Imagine making our relations with the wind-ruffling surface of waters curling round the feet of a Sand Hill and the red-winged blackbird who rests there for a moment in the space-in-between of the wetland. Imagine making our relations with the play of light and shadow across a mountain face and the mischievous eyes of the coyote who wanders up from the plains to the precipice to see what she might be there. Imagine that we might hear the voice of deep time in the stories we are told, might be in and of that voice, yielding, submitting to its harmonies and its grace notes—and conjoining with them.

6

AFTER THE FIRE, A STILL SMALL VOICE

with Vershawn A. Young

The following chapter began with the exchange of letters written between November 2010 and late January 2011 between Vershawn Ashanti Young and me. Vershawn and I met in Chicago one winter at a conference on race and writing centers at the University of Illinois-Chicago. Probably, you too have had the experience of meeting someone and having the sense that you have been given, quite suddenly and unexpectedly, the gift of a chance meeting—an opportunity for a friendship deep and kind and challenging in the best sense.

Friendships require work, and, in truth, the work of friendship, like the work demanded by all our relations, is integral to the possibility of going on together; the necessity for doing the work never ends. It is a mark of the authenticity of the care that animates all sorts of relationships when this work feels joyful even in the hardest moments. In the case of transracial friendships, I think, that joy may develop more slowly, as we learn how to believe that we can lean in toward one another without leaning unduly on one another: that together we can resist the power racism possesses to distort, subvert, and ultimately destroy relationships that transgress established racial order.

When I first conceived of Vershawn (Vay) playing a role in the writing of this book, I imagined him writing a foreword.

When I asked him, though, he declined. He recalled Keith Gilyard's response to him following a similar request, in which Keith urged him to allow his work to stand on its own. Vay said I needed to allow my work to stand and questioned why I might need or want the kind of endorsement a foreword typically signifies for my book from a person of color. Vay never said he wouldn't help with the book, but he thought a foreword was not the way.

These are the kinds of conversations we have every now and again: the kind that stop you in your tracks and make you think long and hard about what you are doing and how and why.

I thought for a while about Vay's point and decided he was right: that I was wrong to look to him or to any person of color to offer an imprimatur of my work's legitimacy. The book needed to stand on its own. But I kept on thinking beyond this conclusion. I thought about the strands of the book that trace possibilities for care, for affiliative relations across racial lines, for mutual engagement and the embrace of challenge such engagement offers, and for love as the question that begins, but can never conclude or resolve, the struggle for racial justice. I went back to Vay and asked him to write with me, to coauthor a chapter in which we might both describe the potential and the challenges of transracial alliance and friendship, but also enact or embody the work those potentials and challenges demand of us. I suggested that we write letters to one another and include them as an epistolary chapter to conclude the manuscript, and he graciously agreed.

The letters we wrote were deliberately personal, although we both knew we were writing for an audience beyond each other. We didn't talk too much about this choice, but it is my belief that we wrote as we did because both of us know that racism does not confine itself to the public spaces of our lives, but conditions our experiences across boundaries between professional and personal, public and private spheres. Both of our working lives are shaped by our shared conviction that to behave as if our struggles with racism are confined either to the personal or the professional spheres of our lives is to represent ourselves, our commitments, and our understanding of racial formation and the power of racism within and across systems and institutions, inadequately and dishonestly. But we have also written personally, I think, because we know not only that this is what the work looks like—moving along perspectival horizons and fields of experience fluidly and dynamically—but this is what the work is. It demands of us that we resist both the external pressure and the inward desire to hide oneself (as if one could, in any case). Antiracist activism, antiracist pedagogy, and transracial friendship and alliance call us all to recognition and acknowledgment that race matters, that racism is real, and that these realities demand address wherever we are: at home, at work, in our communities—within and in service of the relationships we hold dear.

As we reread the letters and talked about them together, Vay and I realized that in writing them each of us had taken up, implicitly at least, big questions. These questions, we believe, may be at some level unresolvable, but must be asked and continuously engaged by antiracist activists as an integral part of the work we do in our communities, our classrooms, and our lives. These, we thought, were not so much questions of the sort one might find on a test or might Google to find an answer. The questions around which the letters were composed stood more as queries, and the letters themselves as meditations.

When it comes to the work of antiracism, there are seasons of rage—times of witness when anger seems a most rational response. Peace and civil rights activist Barbara Deming once noted a distinction, however, between that rage that seeks the absence or death of an Other and that concatenation of anger and love which "is the concentration of one's whole being in the determination: this must change" (n.d.). Deming wrote further of the nesting of rage and love within one another, noting that "only if we accept the presence of ambivalence in the most loving encounters does truth become . . . that which supports evolving human nature in the midst of antagonisms, because these antagonisms call for conscious insight rather than for moralistic repression." There is much to be learned from a long lean into the burn of rage to discern its sources. But if we are to keep on keeping on, I think, we must also lean into and attend to more still moments—moments when, in company with one another, we can burn with conviction and, at the same time, dare to explore the dimensions of ethical (that is to say, thick) relations and to inquire with and for one another more quietly and with care. This is the work of query and meditation.

My knowledge of queries emerges from my involvement in Quaker faith communities. In this context, queries are designed to invite both individual and collective discernment: to test the ways and degrees to which we live the principles we espouse, to offer spiritual and intellectual challenge, and to encourage ongoing vision and revision of perception, consciousness, and action. The point of queries understood in these ways is not to answer them and be done. The point is to stay in consideration of the complex matters that queries raise. Queries function in some way as a guide that does not show you the way, but supports you as you find your own way. Because of their openness, queries invite seekers or learners to return over and over to them, leaning into their challenges anew, revising and reframing meditations stimulated by them.

Vershawn and I offer the following queries and our letters as examples of the ways in which friends and allies within multiracial antiracist activist communities might practice discernment together; might recognize and acknowledge difference while seeking understanding; might talk well and deeply together and stay with the possibility, as well as the limits, of love, through challenge and disagreement. As is the way with correspondence, readers will note that in some cases only one letter takes up a query, while in others the letters unfold as a more extended dialogue around a query. The letters are interrelated across queries so that readers may also notice the ways in which themes or strands reappear and may be woven into a single letter or letters.

Antiracist activists share, I believe, a collective desire for racial justice. We are as susceptible as any other community, however, and perhaps more so, to dispute and to the possibility of being driven apart, our alliances shattered by differences in the kind and quality of our convictions. There are no safe spaces in which to talk about race and racism. In truth, I often think that safety—emotional, spiritual, and intellectual safety, I mean—is not a condition conducive to meaningful antiracist labors. We need conditions in which we can challenge and be challenged, change and be changed. We need conditions in which we can engage with and for one another. To use queries well, as to work with one another well, we need to offer one another serious, compassionate commitments to honesty, forgiveness, confidentiality, clarity, and responsiveness. To the extent that we enact this kind of an offer (or appeal, in the rhetorical sense), we can create shelter spaces where we may not be safe, but where we know we are not alone and will not be cast out. The shelter spaces and the discipline of collective discernment that is possible within them sustain collective antiracist action, even as they nurture and sustain friendship, care, camaraderie, and solidarity.

QUERY

What role does shame play in our engagement with or resistance to the work of antiracism? Do we recognize and acknowledge our sense of shame without becoming submerged in those feelings? Do we work to convert shame to conviction, energy, and will to claim and enact agency in our activism?

Meditation on Shame and on Living in and against a Raced-White Skin

Dear Vay,

You wrote something once that grabbed me, that stayed with me—words that linger and unhinge me just a little bit as you write that you also might be perceived as being unhinged for writing them. You wrote:

I ain't no homeboy—though I long to be and would do anything short of killing to gain that identity—I'm not ghetto enough for the ghetto. Because I'm not a white boy, I'm not white enough for white folks. And because I wasn't born into the middle class, I'm not completely accepted by the mainstream. And sometimes, if you can believe it, I'm not ghetto enough for white folks! The psychoemotional pain that this liminal existence creates, the pain of negotiating multiple cultural and racial worlds, is far too great for many. I've been doing it a long time and have been able to cope only by transforming my personal problem into an intellectual one. In some ways, I'm chipping away at the burden. But far too many are not able to do this. And why should they have to? (2007, xvi)

When first I read these words, they grabbed onto me because they reminded me of my brother, of Rick's experience of being stuck in-between, never white enough and never red enough, and of the reality that he has only found in rare moments ways to study his situation, his experience, as a means of surviving and thriving within it. The pain of living his liminality and, for me, the pain of witnessing his struggles and knowing—*knowing*—that I have played an active role in producing his pain and enforcing his liminality if for no other reason than that as a white sister I stood for the untraversable boundary—have been nearly unbearable, have shaped our separate yet intertwined lives, our separate yet intertwined racial performances, in unbearable ways. Crazy-making ways. And both my brother and I have a little bit of crazy going on.

But these words you penned touched me in another way as well, raised right up out of the racial aquifer of my own sense of self, another truth—not an analogous experience, but a related sense or feeling. For as long as I can remember I have loathed—*hated*—the fact of my own whiteness. I've yearned, dreamed, begged God to make me something else, somebody else, to give me a way out of my skin and all the historical and right-now baggage that attends possessing or at least occupying this skin.

When I was a little girl, I read a book called *All-of-a-Kind Family*. As an adult, I read the title of that book alongside my childish love of the story it tells and just have to smile a bit. Of course, that was my dream: to be part of an all-of-a-kind family. But my dream wasn't for all of us to be white; it was for all of us to be Indian, with Rick. Anyway, in this book, there are five little girls, sisters, in a poor immigrant family—a Jewish family. I read that book over and over and over again; I drank it in; I dreamed that book. I yearned for us all to be Jewish. Maybe becoming Jewish was an attainable transformation, I thought. I took a candelabra and put it in our window, imagining it to be a reasonable approximation of a Menorah, and set the candles alight—until my dad found it and dressed me down for coming close to setting the curtains on fire and burning down the house.

A few years later, my dad, a pianist, became the faculty advisor for a black student singing group on campus: the Gospeleers. Rick and I waited impatiently for every concert. We *loved* that group, loved their music, loved the students who sang with the group—who played with us and teased us and lifted us up with their voices, their songs. Every year, my dad hosted a picnic for the Gospeleers at our home. Rick and I *loved* those picnics. My dad had two baby grand pianos in his music room. The Gospeleers would crowd around those pianos to sing, and the beauty of their music was unbearable.

Rick and I would race between the music room where we listened, enthralled, and the basement, where we watched the old beams on which the floors above rested bend and shake in time with the dancing feet of the singers above. "To be young, gifted and black / Oh what a precious dream / To be young gifted and black / Open your heart to what I mean," they sang, and I did, or I tried as hard as I could to open my heart. "When you feel really low / Yeah, there's a great truth you should know / When you're young, gifted and black / Your soul's intact." I tried. And I knew, *knew*, my soul was not, in fact, intact. It couldn't be, for I was torn apart by the history of my skin (even then I knew), by the ways in which I belonged, capitalized on my belonging, and wished with all my heart to not belong to my skin. I wanted so much to be black. And Rick did too, I know. If we were black, we'd be an all-of-a-kind-family with the Gospeleers. We'd belong with them and they with us. My soul would be intact and Rick's too.

There are times, lots and lots and lots of times, when I am moved by what I see and hear of whiteliness to howl, to shake with rage, to sob at the impotence of my words and my activism. I am not healed, Vay. I hate my skin. Neither Rick nor I would ever escape our skins, however. We would be, are still, caught in spaces-in-between and not in the same spaces-in-between, but in liminalities that are interrelated yet separate, separated from one another and also from our peoples—those who claim us as well as those with whom we most yearn for affiliation.

Many years ago, before I went back to graduate school, I spent quite a bit of time in Japan working as an actor with the avant-garde Japanese director, Tadashi Suzuki. One day, a friend of mine, who worked as a translator for Suzuki-San, told me that he had been asked to translate during a press interview with the premiere Butoh dancer at that time, Yoko Ashikawa. I don't know how much you know about Butoh. In brief, Butoh is an avant-garde dance method(s) and form(s) that developed in Japan after World War II and in particular during the student movements of the late fifties and sixties. Sometimes referred to as the dance of the dark soul, Butoh explores the depths of human feeling and experience—sorrow and absurdity, sexuality and anguish, the body as comedy and tragedy. My friend, whom knew I was fascinated by Butoh, invited me to attend the interview. Ashikawa spoke of the catastrophic dimensions of human tragedy and of the necessity of mourning those aspects of identity, culture, connectedness to history, to tradition, that are lost forever to the boundless universe. I understood her to be describing in metaphorical terms the nuclear holocausts at Hiroshima and Nagasaki. I understood also that Ashikawa experienced her dance not as the singular performance of an individual, but as the performance of collective mourning—the cry of a people and a people's search for meaning in the face of tragedy. She said that when she dances, it is as if she throws away her limbs to the universe without expectation of their return. And in this act of sacrifice, of hope and hopelessness, of faith and faithlessness, she seeks the bottommost point of mourning, the deepest place of sorrow. For only by dancing there, Ashikawa said, is healing possible.

I have thought about Ashikawa's words for years, mulling them over, feeling their power, reaching, stretching to understand, to make sense of them in the context of my own lived experience, my own personal history, and the history of my people. For me, running somewhere beneath the work I do, whether in writing or teaching, parenting, or being a daughter, a sister, or a friend, is this sense, this feeling I learned from Ashikawa: to the extent that all of us mourn—and we must mourn, I believe—what racism has done to us all, I understand that the dance of peoples of color is and must be different from mine—that the range of destructive, dehumanizing conditions that lead to identity formation in the crucible of racism have qualitatively different and greatly magnified effects on peoples of color than they do on whites. But I understand that whites must also dance, must also mourn, and through mourning, heal. We whites must do something more than watch and shake our heads, tsk tsk tsking the mourning and the rage of peoples of color. We must now allow ourselves to feel the weight of loss, in all its dimensions, that racism has caused us—to our material and spiritual lives as well as to our personhood. We human beings belong to one another and because we do we bear responsibility not only for the impact of our own choices on one another, but also for the choices others have made and continue to make in our name. Whites, I believe, need to offer a dance of reparation absent the hope that we could ever give enough to compensate either for the history of racism or for our own complicity in that history. And it can't be guilt (that oh-gosh-I'm-sorry-now-let's-move-on kind of affect) that drives this dance so much as shame. We should feel shame. And the work should be not so much as to avoid or squelch feelings of shame as they emerge in white consciousness, but to acknowledge and discern how we might best move given the fact of our shame— how we might dance at the bottom of our own mourning.

We've talked before about how compelling I find Elspeth Probyn's work. Her book, Vay, is so good (*Blush: The Faces of Shame*). In it, Probyn posits shame as a productive relational force. If guilt is an effect of choices badly made and a temporary condition attached to a social moment that is merely a moment, if guilt is a sensation through which one can pass (perhaps more easily with a brief acknowledgment and apology), shame is a feeling that remains, Probyn says. Shame is the emotional product of interest, of the arrest of "our intense attachment to the world, our desire to be connected with others, and the knowledge that, as merely human, we will sometimes fail in our attempts to make those connections." "When we feel shame," she continues, "it is because our interest has been interfered with but not canceled out. The body wants to continue being interested, but something happens to 'incompletely reduce' that interest" (2005, 15). Guilt, Probyn notes, is easy and temporary, but "shame lingers deep within the self. Being shamed is not unlike being in love. The blush resonates with the first flush of desire. It carries the uncertainty about oneself and about the object of love; the world is revealed anew and the skin feels raw. Shame makes us quiver" (2). Shame is less an effect of surrender or exposure than it is the experience of the incompleteness of love and the reading of that incompleteness back against the self such that one is forced to wonder whether "there [is] something inimical in oneself which keeps love from reaching completion" (Hegel quoted in Probyn, 3). Shame is both an effect and a producer of terror that we have been abandoned in some desolate place, beyond the reach and care of humanity; shame, says Probyn, is a sign of our fragility (3).

This explication of shame resonates powerfully for me. I feel it not as a destructive force, but as a life and love force, productive, deeply invested with desire for relationship. I think, Vay, that those of us who are white especially need to recognize that our shame (and the dance of shame that might constitute white antiracism) is as comedic as tragic, as absurd as studied, as infused with joy as with anguish. As counterintuitive as such a claim may seem to those who see shame as a destructive affect or emotion, shame, I think, is necessary and productive. Shame, thus conceived, teaches the kind of humility that might enable us to stay with the question, to stay with and for one another, to stay at the table. Shame is, I think, for me (and I believe for white antiracists, generally) the condition of the joint at which our lives as raced beings are articulated. And learning to dance there at the joint is, I think, the enabling condition for love that subverts the rules of racial standing—love for Rick, my brother, and for you, my friend. It neither solves nor resolves; it is unspeakable—as filled with laughter and light as with despair. It dances without expectation of return.

QUERY

Are we all alert in our transracial relationships to those moments when we begin to enact color-blind ideology? Do we acknowledge the pressure on all of us to perform whiteliness against one another and against ourselves? Do we acknowledge the pressure whiteliness exerts on all of us in service of preserving a racist status quo?

Meditation on Whiteliness and Silence

Dear Frankie:

It was serendipitous reading your opening chapters because I had been reading at the same time, preparing for class, James Baldwin's essay "White Man's Guilt," and reading the following words, that might as well be my own: "I have often wondered, and it is not a pleasant wonder, just what white Americans talk about with one another. I wonder this because they do not, after all, seem to find very much to say to *me*, and I concluded long ago that they found the color of my skin inhibiting" (1985, 410; italics in original).

Oh, I hate the silence that race breeds! How it becomes the cat that takes white people's tongues when I point to completely obvious racism and they say, "Ignore it. That wasn't about being black. That was about class." They're willing to accept any other cause for some injustice or experience, as long as it ain't about race, Frankie. I told you after reading the opening chapters that it seemed you are writing self-consciously to these white people, to the goodly ones, the whitely whites. And thank God someone is. For many of my whitely acquaintances, the whitely people I meet, often feel immobilizing racial guilt. "And," to quote from Baldwin, "to have to deal with such people can be unutterably exhausting, for they," he says, "with a really dazzling ingenuity, a tireless agility, are perpetually defending themselves against charges which one . . . has not really, for the moment, made." But what's so ironic, Frankie, is, as Baldwin says, "One does not have to make them [the charges]. . . . The record is there for all to read. It resounds all over the world. It might as well be written in the sky." And what you're doing here, in this book, for white people, is echoing Baldwin's wish "that Americans— white Americans—would read, for their own sakes, this record and stop defending themselves against it. Only then will they be enabled to change their lives" (1985, 410).

And isn't that the point? Isn't that one of the reasons why you're writing to white people? But aren't you also writing to me? Of course. You're also writing to that black administrator who questioned whether your mother should have been teaching, had the right to teach, the black experience in film. You're asking that we all take a look. Find no easy answers. But, all the same, interrogate.

Sure, I'm taking this personally. I have to. You quote me, from my book, the anguish I feel at being black, the desire I had (oh, Lord, the desire I have!) to be white, a whiteness Baldwin, in his famous essay "Price of the Ticket" explains: "The price of the black ticket is involved—fatally—with the dream of becoming white" (1985, xiv). He explains the danger in this desire, one that connects people of color, to your whitely readers: "This is not possible," Baldwin cautions, "partly because white people are not white: part of the price of the white ticket is to delude themselves into believing that they are" (1985, ivx).

So, I hear in your pages Baldwin's command, "White man, hear me!" I hear these words with a complex difference. The white man who should hear isn't really white, surely not only white, he's also whitely-black, whitely-Latin, whitely-Iranian, and he really isn't a he, surely not only a he, but also she, or a him-she—it's all of us who are on the path, the only path, I say, that America holds out to us, particularly in school, in education, the path to become white. What you want us to hear about our collective racial history, and our personal ones, I find, yes, again, in the words of Baldwin, whom I'll quote at length and end:

> History, as nearly no one seems to know, is not merely something to be read. And it does not refer merely, or even principally, to the past. . . .. [History] is literally *present* in all that we do. It could scarcely be otherwise, since it is to history that we owe our frames of reference, our identities, and our aspirations. And it is with great pain and terror that one begins to realize this. In great pain and terror one begins to assess the history which has placed one where one is and formed one's point of view. In great pain and terror because, therefore, one enters into battle with that historical creation, Oneself, and attempts to recreate oneself according to a principle more humane and more liberating; one begins the attempt to achieve a level of maturity and freedom which robs history of its tyrannical power, and also changes history." (1985, 410; italics in original)

Let's change history, my friend.

QUERY

Do we acknowledge and are we reflective about the ways in which racial identity complicates transracial relations? Do we think carefully and critically about our readiness in every context in which we may be called to lead or teach? Do we reach across racial lines with humility and tenderness to help one another learn and grow?

Meditation on Teaching and Leading across Racial Lines

Dear Vay,

My mom told me recently that she regrets not having stayed in that conversation with the black administrator. She said that the cost of her refusal to stay fell on the students, who wanted and needed courses focused on their history and taught in ways that empowered. One of the struggles for white academics, it seems to me, is to recognize the extent to which our advanced degrees, the long-cultivated habits of mind we possess and take pride in, all our book learning, does not, in fact, prepare us for the work of antiracism. Of course, my mom was qualified to teach black experience in film—at some level. She had studied, had labored long and hard at those studies, had been taught by some of the finest historians in the country, had been certified by a fine university. She knew her stuff. She knew *her* stuff. But, as a white woman, to teach *black experience?* In what way would all that book learning prepare her to do that?

I've tried imagining a different title for that course; what if she had retitled it Representations of Blacks in American Film? In some ways, I do suspect that the course, titled in this way, would not have raised questions in exactly the same way, but the concerns would have nagged, perhaps, nonetheless. Could my mom, under any circumstances, have addressed the critical matter of *impact* as a matter of lived experience? Of course, she and her students could have read the accounts of black actors who were denied roles in those films so that white actors could play at being people of color, or the accounts of black actors who did perform in the films, accounts of black directors and producers. They could have read about the critical reception of such films in black communities and the reviews of black critics. They could have read *about* impact. But would this have helped my mom or her students to the address the matter of the impact of those representations on her students? Maybe the question that black administrator was trying to pose to my mom had to do not with her qualifications to teach the history of race and representation in America, or of film history, but to teach her students—the young adults gathered in that classroom each week. Maybe that was the question my mom was just unprepared in that moment so long ago to hear and to which she was unprepared to respond.

One of the critical points I'm trying to make in the book, Vay, is that no one knows instinctively or ontologically how to enact antiracism as activism, as pedagogy, or both. Our degrees and honors and certifications, valuable as they may be, do not prepare us for this work. This is a way of thinking, being, acting that must be learned—and that can't be mastered, certified, or credentialed. The question of whether or how we are or might be prepared as antiracists to organize, to act, to teach, is particularly vexed, I think, for white activists and teachers. I believe I have a particular responsibility to address racism well and meaningfully in my community, in the classrooms where I teach, and in the writing centers I administer.

And one of the key elements in all of the antiracism trainings I've participated in has been preparation to step up as a white person, to take responsibility for opening the conversation with other whites, for teaching—to not expect or rely on peoples of color to do all the work when it comes to resisting racism. But the trainings I've attended have been activist-centered and I'm not sure any of them have taken up the challenge faced by my mom, a challenge I now face as well. I teach in multiracial classrooms. What is it that qualifies me to teach about racism, to teach resisting racism to students of color?

Let me tell you a story or two from this semester. There are fifteen students in my writing-center theory and practice course. Of those, five are American students of color (one of whom is a first-generation immigrant) and two are international students of color. One of the books on our reading list is Harry Denny's new book *Facing the Center*, and a few weeks ago we were discussing that text in class. Jenna (I've given her a pseudonym), who identifies as a black woman, raised her hand. "This book really seems like it was written for white people," she said. I don't know if you've read it yet, Vay, but Harry's book takes up identity and difference in the writing center with chapters on race, ethnicity, class, nationality, and sexual orientation that introduce readers to current theories of identity, to the complexity of identities as they are performed in the context of a writing center, and to ways of thinking about teaching/tutoring among and across diverse identities. "Say more, Jenna," I prompted. "Why does it seem that way to you?" "Well," said Jenna, "I don't need all this instruction. This is the world I live in. It's multicultural all the time. All of my friends, all of my family, every community I belong to—I just already know all this stuff."

I'm not sure I did a very good job of answering Jenna, Vay. For one thing, and this I did tell her, she may well be right. It may well be true that Harry's book is written to straight, white, middle-class, third- or fourth-generation Americans. There is this way in which I am aware when I am teaching about race and racism that the students in my classroom to whom what and how I am teaching will be new are the white students. I'm trying all the time to teach well without recentering whiteness. I tried to explain this to Jenna, with the rest of the class looking on. I am aware of this tension and of the degree to which I might be teaching, simultaneously, two different subjects. I am aware that even as I am teaching my white students about racism, I am inviting students of color both to bear witness and to subject what I say and how I say it, to subject me, really—my antiracist praxis—to their critical gaze. I'm trying to shift the center from whiteness, from whiteliness, to performative resistance where the actor is white. And I'm aware all the time of how fine these lines are, how tenuous my claims, my justifications, are.

But there is more than this to say and I didn't say it all to Jenna on that day in class. I thought, but didn't say, that she may well be right in suggesting that she doesn't need the instruction Harry offers in his book. Jenna is a young woman who may well do a little rocking of the world someday. She wants to be a lawyer. She's deep and thoughtful, deliberative, and wise. Jenna, in particular, already possesses a keen insight into the racial dynamics of social relations and an extraordinary ability to write into and against the force of racism. But even Jenna might not have it all down, might not know everything she'll need or want to know to *engage* critically, meaningfully, in a performative anti-racism. Do Harry or I have a role in teaching her this? Could we teach her? What would be our qualifications to teach Jenna? And, truthfully, not all students of color have seen what Jenna has seen, know what Jenna knows, are able to act, to perform, as Jenna is able to do. What of them?

Here's another story. Robert (not his real name) is a Puerto Rican American who spent his childhood in the Bronx, moving to Lincoln with his mom in high school. He is taking my class this semester, but has already started working in the writing center. One day in class, we were working on tutoring practice in a fishbowl kind of arrangement. Robert and the writer with whom he was consulting were sitting in the center of a circle of chairs so that all the other students were observing the consultation. To open the conversation, Robert, who had quickly read through the text in his hand, said something like, "Well, you've got a good start here. Of course there are a lot of grammatical errors, and we'll get to those as we talk through your work." I stopped the consultation and asked Robert to talk about why he had chosen to open the conversation in that way. "Well," said Robert, "I'm aware, I mean, I have this instinct, that sometimes when writers come into the writing center and see me, with my brown skin, and they hear me speak, they think I'm not qualified to teach them anything. So, I want to make sure they know right off that I see their mistakes. I want them to know I'm not going to miss anything." "Oh my God!" I thought to myself, "How am I going to speak into this moment?!?!"

I told Robert that I wanted to honor both his sense, his instinct, about how he is sometimes read by writers in the writing center and his courage in naming that reading aloud to the class. I cannot, I told the class, in good faith, say that Robert is wrong. I know, because of how students try to schedule appointments, because of what students write to me in emails, because of what students write in consultation evaluations, that there are student-writers who doubt the competence of the consultants of color with whom they work. I said that, for me, what needs to be front and center in any consultation is student learning. I want consultants to make deliberate and reflective choices about when and how they address the problem of error in service of student learning. This does not mean, I went on to say, overlooking error, but choosing carefully when and how to address it. On the other hand, I am aware—have, in fact, quite consciously constructed a situation in which student-writers might unlearn some of their notions about who is or isn't a writer, who is or isn't a teacher or tutor, about their own competencies and those of other writers, through their encounters with a diverse staff of writing center consultants—a staff that includes writers of color, international ELL consultants, and queer consultants. I told Robert, with the rest of the class looking on, the story of Elijah and Passover. I told him how curious I had felt about that Passover ritual of leaving a door ajar for Elijah and about how I had gone looking for stories of Passover to learn why that door might be left open. I told them about the Rabbinical accounts I read and how so many of them included not only the story of Elijah's return as a heralding of the coming of the Messiah, but also the story of leaving the door ajar so Christians could see that the Jews were not drinking the blood of Christian babies.

I told Robert that, for me, there is a metaphorical kinship between the practice of leaving the door open for Others to gaze in—to unlearn the distrust, the hate they know—and his practice of pointing to error as a means of demonstrating his competence in the face of unsupported, discriminatory doubt. These choices are understandable and they ought to make all of us tremble in some sense; ought to shake our complacency about the "safety" and "comfort" of the places where we dwell both literally and figuratively. I think I made reference to your article "Momma's Memories and the New Equality," which we had read previously. The challenge, for all of us, I said, is to find ways to expose and trouble, to shake down those wicked preconceptions of (in)competence, for example, that are attached to racial identity (or other identities marked in the dominant everyday as Other) without reenacting or recapitulating other similarly dismissive, discrediting, or disempowering practices—without using "the master's tools." I did not try to tell Robert how to do that. After all this work, Vay, after all this thinking and talking and writing and learning, unlearning and relearning, I still do not know what to tell Robert.

I didn't say, but I know it's true, that I have learned the ways of thinking, speaking, writing about which I write here, and which I've been teaching all semester in my writing-center theory and practice class, from peoples of color in the antiracism movement. I've learned by watching, by listening carefully, by being called out and leaning in to learn from those moments. The epistemology and rhetoric constituted by storytelling and the historicizing of story, by decentering, nuancing, and by thinking and acting in and through a long now—these are conceptual frames and practices of which I would have no knowledge and with which I would have no experience were it not for the kindness, the generosity, and the instruction of peoples of color within the antiracism movement. I've tried to give voice to that which I've observed, tried, and tested. I've tried to pass forward in the book that which I've learned to other whites. I think I have to pass these matters forward to my students of color as well and I have to learn to do this, somehow, with an awareness of, a responsiveness to, their multiple and various lived experiences. I have to do this even as I resist appropriating either those experiences or those forms of intervention and resistance that must belong to peoples of color. And I think I have to do this without reenacting whiteliness—without wearing those washed-out, worn-out, nasty old garments of paternalism, "*noblesse oblige*," condescension. I have to keep thinking about, keep questioning, my qualifications to teach my students of color well without "throwing up my hands" or abdicating my responsibility to *act*, to be an *actor*, not a player.

QUERY

Do we seek together to understand the conditions that make trust possible in transracial friendships, partnerships, and alliances? Do we give trust generously on one hand, and recognize that trust is earned on the other? Do we seek always to act with integrity in our relations with one another and do we talk well and deeply with one another about what acting with integrity might mean?

Meditations on Trust

Dear Frankie:

I knew when I first met you, when I heard you give that keynote speech at the Race and Writing Center Conference at UIC, when you put your own personal history right out in public in the service of antiracism, when you described your brother Rick's experience with racism, of being called a nigger, a word you said without restraint, but certainly with the ethics of care, in the service of sharing that experience, to make the problems plain, yes, I knew right then, on that night in early March 2008, that I wanted you to be my friend and colleague. And I told you so after your talk, didn't I? I told you with perhaps too much of the honesty that has gotten me into trouble too often, told you with a caveat drenched in fear that I want to have coffee with you, maybe brandy, to get to know you better, to join this work you're doing. Then I told you: "But I don't trust white people!" Don't trust the antiracists. Actually, only the antiracists. And as I write to you now, I feel the same way, the same trepidation, and the same anxiety about my relationships with white liberals.

Think about it: to say that I don't trust white people who are ultra right winged, the Christian conservative type, the Tea Partiers, or those who voted for the Kentucky neosegregationist Rand Paul, or those who would superimpose the image of a chimpanzee over Michelle Obama's face and publish it on the Internet, or those adherents of Rush Limbaugh, a man who, on the very night of Obama's election, said "I want him to fail," and said more than that, Frankie, he said, "*We are being told that we have to hope he succeeds, that we have to bend over, grab the ankles, bend over forward, backward, whichever, because his father was black, because this is the first black president*"—to say I don't trust these ones, someone who would spew intertwined homophobic, anti-black criticism, invoking the very fear mongering and racism that ignite lynch mobs and that undergird racist ideologies, including institutional ones, is to state the obvious, to be so annoyingly redundant.

Those types are not trying to cultivate my trust, couldn't care less about it. But you are, aren't you, friend? As also I aim to do in reciprocal return. So I said my thing, and I don't now remember what you said. But I remember what you did. The next day after I gave my solo performance of *Your Average Nigga*, when a white woman gave an anecdote about being the chair—the chair!—of a search committee that did not hire a black female as a writing teacher because the black interviewee said "he don't" once during her interview, you spoke up. Many in the audience were, to my mind, insufficiently enraged, but you challenged, asking the woman her thoughts on Joseph William's essay "The Phenomenology of Error." You said we all make errors, particularly in speech. Why was this woman's mishap so glaring, so big that it cost her the job? And you pointed to the very racialized thinking. Oh, why don't I just say it? The very racist thinking of so many white liberals. That woman actually was wringing her hands, as so many liberals do. Then throw them up and say, "What do we do?" As if she were the very personification of conjugation, had perfect control over all her verbs, her nouns. But none of us do. Not even when we write. Not even when tutors and copyeditors go over the pages. That woman's anecdote illustrates ingrained racial thinking, the very kind that you're writing about in the book, the kind that happens every day in coffee shops, at business meetings, in writing centers, in writing classrooms. You spoke up! And you keep speaking up, and out!

Oh, I remember, friend, what you did. And I see what you do. I remember we exchanged numbers and emails. I remember we talked. We met at conferences with no political agenda (but we do want to change the world, don't we?) other than to hang. (What fun!) And I remember coming for visits to your home for the same reasons, meeting Mike, and Grace, and Lucy, and Dan, and your mom, too. I remember, and I see. And now you've written this book. And I find myself excited—and anxious—oh, so anxious—all over again. I'm excited because your book invites white liberals, well-meaning, good-hearted people, to listen, not just to you, but, most importantly, to themselves, to their personal histories, to the stories that drive their beliefs, interrogate their own goodliness, whiteliness. Let me take your advice, too, here, and tell you a small bit of my own history.

When I say to you that I don't trust the antiracists, I'm not trying to put you on the spot, to put a burden on you to fulfill my racial expectations. Never may that happen! I'm saying what you say, I think. That it's a partnership, a deeply reciprocal relationship, where we stick with it: maintain the work despite the obstacles, and despite the (fill in the blank). I'm saying that in my experience, my so-called antiracist colleagues and friends have left too soon and too often. And my mother's words haunt me: "Don't trust nobody. Don't trust white people." She says that, Frankie, because she believes that when I'm not around, not looking, my white friends will slip up around not-so-well-meaning white people, people they have access to in informal, personal relationships, perhaps people with power, and repeat something I said or did that these other whites find offensive or too black or something, and then I'd be in trouble. She's scared for me to be friends with white people, Frankie.

I remember Momma pointing out a scene in the movie version of *Roots*, when Kizzie was sold to another master. Now Kizzie was a slave, of course, but she believed she was the friend of the master's daughter, whom she'd play with, talk to, and love. She made the master's daughter promise not to sell her. But not long after the promise, Kizzie was sold by the father, the master.

And the daughter did nothing. Said nothing. Looked on with indifference. Didn't even say, "Daddy don't." Nothing! These are the kinds of stories Momma thinks of when she advises me not to trust white people. And, I have my own. Not from other people's nonfiction, but from my own life. The white people I long to trust, to love, indeed have trusted, have loved, are the ones who profess "multiculturalism," that "racism is bad," that "feminism is important." But I see often that they mean this theoretically. And I'm not critiquing them for being imperfect, fallible. Who gets it right all the time? Not me. So who?

But friends are the ones closest to you, next to family. And their slights cut deep. I know this. What I'm saying is that in my experience they don't consistently stick with it. They certainly haven't stuck with me! They'd rather I be quiet, don't start that racial trouble, act right, tow the row, at least wait until *they're* indignant. Then I can join *them*. Ain't that something?! Or, get this, they pull rank with their racial privilege. And attempt to tell me, "Hey buddy, watch it, I'm white," just before I tell them to go to hell. And, it's like, "Momma told me so, didn't she?" And I resist this, want to keep trying. So I do, but with an open acknowledgment of my own stuff, my own history with race, my own distrust and the reasons why right here, laid out on the table.

Dear Vay,

Thank you for writing about trust. I think about my years in the movement, about the white folks who have come and gone, and know, just *know* that the necessity of earning trust has seemed too much for some, too hard and too time consuming and too unfair given how good we all try to be. I think perhaps that one of the characteristics of whiteliness is a consuming interest in the right-here-right-now; to the extent that one becomes aware of being seen, of the critical gaze of peoples of color, one wants to believe or to demand that the judgment of that gaze be based only on *this moment* absent individual and collective histories, absent memory, and absent the will to make the way, together, toward futures abundant with possibility. As I read your letter, I thought of a lesson I took far too long to learn in my life: whenever anyone says "trust me," run for the hills. Whiteliness does seem to claim trust by fiat. And when that command is not obeyed, too many of us white folks absent ourselves from the work as punishment for peoples of color who have dared to gaze, perhaps, or because the idea of earning something so dear as trust seems too overwhelming?

Perhaps I swerve away from writing directly about trust because I don't know what can righteously be said by whites like me about trust. To write of trust is, perhaps, as Barthes suggests, "to confront the *muck* of language: that region of hysteria where language is both *too much* and *too little*, excessive . . . and impoverished" (1979, 99; italics in original). I am not sure how one could "read the record," lean into history as a white person to learn rather than deny the fact of history's accretion in our individual and collective present tenses and continue to demand trust, command that others trust us, or even believe that trust is possible. Trust, at some level, is beside the point. The point, as you say, is to *do* something, to *act* with integrity, but (and here's the unremarked underneath of *integrity*) without expectation of some return on the investment of *doing, acting*. Too many whites slip away from the work of antiracism, I think, because we have mistakenly acted with the expectation that *gratitude* and *trust* will be our recompense for having acted. Sadly, our departures undo all we have done—all we might do.

I hear your momma's caution to you and think, "Of course, she's right." The way of friends, of comrades, of colleagues is made not in grand pronouncements of care and friendship, of trust, but in the everyday choices made when we are together as well as when we are apart, and even and especially in the face of the truth that we cannot, no matter what, see through one another or ourselves. Barthes again:

> I am caught in this contradiction: on the one hand, I believe I know
> the other better than anyone and triumphantly assert my knowledge

to the other ("I know you—I'm the only one who really knows you!"); and on the other hand, I am often struck by the obvious fact that the other is impenetrable, intractable, not to be found; I cannot open up the other, trace back the other's origins, solve the riddle. Where does the other come from? Who is the other? I wear myself out, I shall never know. (1979, 134)

How much more profound is this experience of *not knowing*, of knowing only that one cannot know, when the impossibility of knowing one another, of seeing right through to the heart, is amplified by histories of racism, by ideologies of race, by racism in the right-here-right-now! Baldwin is right. Barthes continues, "'I can't get to know you' means 'I shall never know what you really think of me.' I cannot decipher you because I do not know how you decipher me" (1979, 134). We really must, I think, let go of our desire to *know* one another as if there is a self distinct from what we *do* in this world. And to undo whiteliness, all of us whitely folks will have to jettison the notion that we can be, ought to be, judged by those qualities of interior self, in spite of what we do (or don't do). We'll have to jettison that sense that the content of our characters could ever exist as freefloating soul matter apart from our actions and inactions, apart from what we say and apart from our silences. We compose our characters as we act with and for one another. There is nothing else available to us but this on which to base love, or trust, or friendship, or alliance.

This is a terrible and terrifying reality—a potentially immobilizing truth. What if I make a mistake?! What of my character when I fail?! But to think in this way is to think as if through every action or inaction one sets some aspect of one's character in stone. We do learn; we do change. We can try to hide our mistakes, carrying them with us as secrets (thinly disguised, whatever we may tell ourselves about how deeply we have hidden them). But there are other choices available to us; we can tell the stories, and by telling, by making those mistakes available to ourselves as well as to the critical gaze of others, learn from them. This, more than trust, for me is the real test of friendship, of alliance, of camaraderie: do we learn with one another?

Oh, My Dearest Frankie:

Over several weeks, I have intermittently labored emotionally and intellectually over my response to the role of trust in anti-racist writing-center and literacy work, a matter about which it seems we disagree. My labor in writing is fueled by a series of self-queries: "Is Frankie prodding me to be clearer about trust? How could I better explain to my friend that trust prompted my first interaction with her and undergirds our very relationship? How do I say to Frankie that without trust, I couldn't be her friend, her colleague? How do I make plain that I would not be able to engage the important project—"to learn from one another"—without knowing she has my back, won't turn on me, will be reliable, will work to build a mutual ethos of interpersonal confidence? These questions began to swirl when I read your statement that "trust, at some level, is beside the point. The point . . . is to *do* something, to *act* with integrity." These questions still swirl because I think of trust differently in this context: it is precisely the point.

But I wonder whether this particular line of reasoning is worth a quibble. And in an earlier draft of this letter I wrote, "Nope, it's not worth it." But after laboring some more, after sitting at the computer far longer than I should because I'm already late for church, after feeling my breath abate as it does when I'm intensely involved in writing, after feeling my forehead wrinkle, mouth clinch, eyes squint, staring at every word I type, trying to be careful, trying to nuance, I've revised my "nope" to "yep." Yep, it's worth an objection.

I see trust at work in our interactions, in these very letters. Would I write to you what I've written, speak so openly and honestly, without trusting you? Uh uh. Surely, not. Trust is the very idea that amplifies for me the key concepts I read in your book, particularly ideas of love and of sticking with it. So I'm going to make a request of you that I hope won't send you running for the hills: "Trust me, Frankie." And, I'm going to make a proclamation: "Friend, I trust you."

Now, what does trust have to do with our antiracism work in the context of literacies, of teaching writing, of educating anyone, especially tutors and future teachers? Allow me to speak into a few of your illustrations and speak on one of my own.

When Robert, the tutor in your writing-center course, rehearses that one of the first things he would say to a writer is that he's going to help her fix her grammatical errors, Robert is trying to build trust. He is, in effect, asking the student to trust him, to have confidence in his abilities to help her with her paper. Of course, I think you were right to be alarmed about how and why he went about building trust, since he is playing into the very racist stereotypes that he wants to subvert. In other words, he's anticipating a racist reading of his abilities based on his ethnic identity. And he is eagerly embracing the burden of racial performance, trying to prove that he's the right type of Puerto Rican, the smart one. But this performance can never appease racism, that unrelenting, bloodthirsty beast! Robert is setting himself up for incessant surveillance and adjudication of his abilities by the very ones he's there to assist. What if he misses the subject/verb agreement in a client's paper, say, not marking where the student uses the construction "criteria is" instead of "criterion is" or "criteria are." Or what if he says to a student, "C'mon in. Let's you and I sit over at this table and talk today" instead of "Let's you and me sit..."? After these two instances, will it then be appropriate for someone to think he fails to catch these errors because he is Puerto Rican? To base his grammar on his race? It certainly shouldn't be. So, Robert is setting up trust on the wrong basis. Instead, trust has to be mutual. He could say to the writer, "We work together on all matters pertaining to your writing. But, of course, the project and the final product are entirely and ultimately yours. I'm here to assist in any way to make that paper sing the way you want it to. I have a few ideas about how that can work. But first, what are the ways you think we can work together?" This opens the opportunity for them both to do what you say, Frankie, to learn together. The trust building is based on mutual respect.

What about Jenna? Jenna's response to Harry's book that her world is already multicultural reflects why it's often hard to bridge the gap of racial understanding between whites and others. She illustrates why trust is hard to build. Let's say for the sake of argument that Jenna knows about all the multicultural points Harry writes about—which is doubtful, but okay. What she can learn, if the book is written for whites, is the same thing I'm learning from yours: why whites have such a difficult time with race, race conversations, and deep self-interrogation when it comes to race. I'm reminded here of Baldwin's admission: "I have often wondered, and it is not a pleasant wonder, just what white Americans talk about with one another" (1985, 410). One of the good outcomes of whiteness studies and of white people being self-reflective, self-analytical, is that the public conversation is being had, thank God. And we all can grow from it. Jenna's not excused from the reading and neither am I. Just as whites are not excused from participating in Black History Month, and looking and learning all they can. Just as men are not excused from Women's History Month, etc. To build trust, we need to take a permanent seat at the table of others, looking and learning, not just for ourselves but for ways to help others and ourselves. Jenna can ask, "How is it that I've come to know these fundamental ideas and others haven't?" As a secondary audience, what is the book offering me? How can the text be useful in my role as tutor?" This is an opportunity to build trust.

To me, Frankie, we *should* work to cultivate trust. I disagree with Momma's advice to me not to trust white people. I prefer to endow my relationships with trust first, rather than making my friends work for it. This isn't blind trust or even naïve. It's a gift. Now, when I encounter words like those from Grimm, I'm skeptical, even though I approached *Good Intentions* with trust. But trust must be cultivated. As you say, "We must do something, act with integrity."

As for you, my friend, I think it's fine that we may occupy different subject positions. You do not have to adopt my view on trust, nor really am I writing this to persuade you to. What's more important to me is the understanding . . . that I need that trust. But for you trust is beside the point. We may disagree, but what you're doing still cultivates that trust, we're still working together and are not at odds, our faiths are mutually influencing. Does trusting mean I won't make a mistake? Will you be perfect? Nope. But I trust that we will work to pursue success even though we will inevitably, sometimes miserably, fail.

My Dear Vay,

I'm not running for the hills at your assertion that you trust me, but I am scared. Partly I'm scared, as you've predicted, because I just know I'm going to fail in small and large ways and feel so much worse about those failures, even as I try to learn from them—because I will be failing you, my friend. I'm less worried about not having your back as I do have that fury inside that drives me—born of years of bearing witness already—than I am about having your back badly or inadequately. I'm scared of flying into battle as if I could speak for you, could speak better on your behalf than you could yourself. I'm scared of you seeing me in those moments when my own facility with the rhetorics of whiteliness erupts. I'm scared of what you'll think of me when white supremacy becomes me and I perform what I abhor, failing to enact those principles I claim.

This morning, though, I lean into this fear, prodded by your letter, to try to discern more fully its dimensions. I play out worst-case scenarios (something I seem to be preternaturally good at). And where I get to is that I do, in fact, trust you too. I trust you to call me out, to call me back to mindfulness, and to stay with me as agent provocateur, and as my dear friend. I remind myself as I allow myself to acknowledge the mutuality of this trust that one of my challenges continues to be resistance to an overreliance on your trust and your good will; my challenge is to take responsibility for my own work, without asking or expecting you to teach me how or to do the work for me. And this, I recognize, points to a fault line. I trust that you will help me, teach me, stay with me; I know I can neither expect nor rely on you to do those things. I'm afraid I'll lean too hard on your trust, taking it for granted, as a right. And I know that your trust of me depends or should depend upon my willingness to do my own work. I gnaw on the fact of this fault line.

When I wrote that trust is beside the point, I should have said that I think white and whitely folks have a complicated and troubling relationship with trust in antiracism work (as well as in refusals or resistance to joining that work). In the context of developing rhetorical readiness to recognize, acknowledge, and resist racism, white and whitely folks must address this relationship in its complexity. My observation, and I suspect yours as well, is that at the early stages of engagement with the matters of race and racism, whites tend to expect trust from peoples of color and to express surprise and outrage when that trust is not forthcoming. To me, this phenomenon seems an effect of the logics of past and present, presence and absence, guilt and innocence. The origins and the worst of racism are firmly located in the past, many of us claim. We were not present at their inception nor were we present or complicit when things were at their worst. Therefore, we are innocent and bear little or no responsibility for things as they were or as they are now (to the extent that racism exists in the present and is an effect of history). If these claims are true, peoples of color have no reason not to trust us. As we continue to think and dialogue about race and racism, we whites may begin to feel that trust ought to be predicated on our intentions, which are, we believe, good and righteous. Failures to garner trust, or refusals to grant trust, become easily available exits from the work of antiracism. Too frequently, it seems to me, we treat the emotional labor of antiracism work as an insurmountable obstacle to meaningful engagement with other (rhetorical, epistemological, intellectual) dimensions of the work.

But even as white engagement with antiracism deepens, as we study more and try with increasing commitment and discipline to think, speak, and act differently, trust remains a complex and troubling matter for us, I believe. There is a competitive edge to white engagement. We begin to search for legitimacy as antiracists by seeking the approbation of our colleagues of color—your fondness, your friendship, your trust. And we seek legitimacy by acting in ways that compare favorably with other whites. We seek to cultivate reputations as good white people, better white people than other white folks, the best white person—the one who *is* trusted. In other words, we continue to live within and perform whiteliness even as we begin to conceive of ourselves as "antiracist."

I wouldn't say this is a matter we talk about much (under the heading of things white people talk about when peoples of color aren't around); who would want to admit to feeling this nasty little desire (with its holier-than-thou edge) to be better than the rest, after all? But this dynamic, this tension, snakes between us, threatening our solidarity with one another as well as with the peoples of color with whom we affiliate. When I wrote that trust was beside the point, Vay, I was thinking of this: if I allow myself to be drawn into a sense of my own legitimacy by virtue of my friendship with you, then you and I have no relationship worth having—not because of anything you've done, but because of me, because of my deceit, my own forked tongue. Mine will be an empty or merely theatrical performance of friendship and of commitment to the work we do together and singly.

I do trust you, Vay, and want so much to be trusted by you. But I can't allow my yearning to be trusted to trump my ongoing labor toward performative antiracism: to enact what I say and write as I speak, write, act. This is what I mean when I say trust is beside the point. For me, the impetus, the driving force for my work as an antiracist educator and activist, has to be an ongoing critique of the (il)logics of racism, an ongoing decentering and nuancing of white implicatedness, of my own implicatedness in those (il)logics, and the intertwined commitment to remember and to imagine alternative futures in the everyday that composes my life. I feel, must feel, I think, your trust of me as a gift and not a reward or an earned wage—as an honor I have no right to expect and for which I have every reason to feel gratitude and awe.

QUERY

Do we take responsibility for transforming racist conditions within the institutions, communities, and systems in and through which we live our lives? Do we accept that responsibility without displacing it onto those who are most subject to racism? Are we alert as we speak or write to those moments when we may reiterate positions or perspectives that reinscribe or reenact implicit or explicit racism? Do we stay, even when staying is hardest—when our own work is the subject of critique?

Meditations on Antiracist Critique

My Dear Frankie:

I've debated whether or not I should give voice to this concern. But I think I must. I read some of the work of our white antiracist colleagues and I am not encouraged to trust. I sigh and distrust. Over the past several years, I've been trying to understand and speak to Nancy Grimm's book *Good Intentions*, which makes strong points against institutional practices that reify racism. Yet, ultimately when it comes to students of difference, particularly of color, she puts the burden on them (similar to the way your student, Robert, embraces the burden). Note what Grimm says: "When I meet with groups of students from traditionally underrepresented groups on my campus, I tell them that the most dangerous assumption they can make, the one that may lead to academic failure, is that the institution is fair. . . . I tell them directly that they will have to work harder and smarter than most students to be successful because our university was not designed with them in mind" (1999, 104).

Oh my God!!!

Frankie, Grimm's book is over ten years old, but I still hear this perspective at conferences and read it in articles. This idea (!) continues to circulate and recirculate in our field and in our communities. The problems with it are many. But two stand out for me. The first is that people of color (in this case, students) have to become responsible for an institution's racism. From this perspective and in this case, it seems as if it is the students' job to master whatever expectations are held out for peoples of color by "dominant" groups—plus way (I say too much) more. It's the old, "You have to work twice as hard to get half as far" line. Okay, I recognize the problem Grimm is pointing out, but her solution is wrong. It breeds further oppression. What if the students are only able to do just as much as students from dominant groups? What if they are only able to meet the expectations the university holds out for all others? Then what? The conversation should start here. Start with working to balance these scales in the institution, not putting further burdens on students.

The other thing Grimm misses is this: What if students from nondominant groups, those whom the university doesn't have in mind, come to school just as prepared as those from dominant groups? What if everything else besides their racial background is exactly the same? Would you still tell the students they have to work harder and smarter? How will working smarter help them overcome the obstacles they continue to face, even though they've spent their entire lives working hard and have no intention not to work hard? You must then address the real problem, alleviating the circumstances that create the imbalance in the first place.

At this moment in her book, Grimm perpetuates a discourse of inequality. "The university doesn't see y'all as equal; so now y'all gotta do way more just to get it to recognize you." Huh?! Why not say, "The university has a responsibility to recognize each person as equal. It has failed to do that consistently, but y'all are not responsible for that failure in any way. And no further burdens should be added to you to try to accommodate that failure. It is part of my responsibility to find ways to support you in meeting the expectations the university has for everybody. You will not have more, if I can help it. As a professor, it is my job to build coalitions in the institution and to speak out and work for changes that will make the experience of students of difference the same as those whom the university welcomes with open arms."

She'd have my trust if she uttered these different words followed by concrete actions.

Dear Vay,

One thing I think of as I read your critique of Grimm's work is that I'm glad you noticed and named a moment that many of us may have read over too easily or read past altogether. I'm sorry it had to be you who noticed and spoke to that moment, though. I feel sorry because of how often it seems we whites depend on peoples of color to offer such critiques and because I know that none of us yet have a good sense of what to do, how to process when critiques like yours come at us. Part of the work I hope we white antiracists will do is to work toward increasing awareness, reflectiveness, and critical engagement with what are really unexamined bits of cant or "common (non)sense."

Here's what I believe: neither meaningful transracial alliances nor authentic multiracial friendships are created by fiat. We do not create these relationships by the desire to do well together. They're developed over time as we think, talk, and act together, as we grapple with contested ideas together, write and revise our individual and collective stories together. You and I have had some time and have, I hope, a lot more time to grow with and for one another and to cultivate our ability to work together. And I'll grant you this: if we cannot trust that we are both committed to taking "a permanent seat at the table," even and especially when we are compelled to make this kind of critique or to receive it, then we can neither bond deeply with one another nor accomplish much together.

I guess what I'm saying is that for white folks taking a permanent seat at the table requires that we be prepared to process the range of conflicting feelings that might overtake us as we engage and are engaged by the contestation that attends the study of race matters. We need to be prepared to stay with the work and with and for one another even and especially when

the conversation gets hard and it feels like our stuff—our thinking, feeling, knowing, learning: our contributions to the work—
is on the line. We need to be courageous in raising the kind of
critique you offer in response to Grimm's book. But I also think
all of us, and maybe especially whites committed to combating
racism, need to be courageous in leaning into those critiques
when they come at our own work. This way of thinking about
published antiracist or antioppression work, in particular, is different than the way we might think about more traditional academic publications. Here the objective ought not to be to have
the last word or to demonstrate through the writing that I am/
you are the biggest and best expert of all on the topic. No, the
object in antiracist writing is to write so that more and more people can join the conversation and so that the conversation continues infinitely or as long as it needs to anyway. When I think
about what courage means in this context, I think it demands
of all of us (but I'm thinking now especially of white folks) not
only intellectual engagement, the willingness to question and
be questioned, to test what we think in the commons, but also
a kind of spiritual and emotional readiness—humility—to learn
and to change in public as we do in private: to let go of our
sense of our published work as the substance of our legacy and
to see, instead, our long lean into learning as the gift we bring
to the labor.

QUERY

*Do we approach our work as antiracists with humility? Do we think
carefully and critically about the quality of our witness and the uses to
which that witness may be put? Are we aware and reflective of the ways
in which racism may inform our willingness to see, to hear, and believe
the testimony of others?*

Meditation on White and Whitely Witness and Testimony

Dear Frankie:

   In this, the last of our epistolary exchange, but certainly not
the end of our engagement with each other and the important

issues raised here, allow me to summarize something I'm still uneasy about. But let me begin my ending statement with an experience that will help me explain. I don't remember telling you this story. I think I meant to, but now is the perfect time, I think.

The day after Barack Obama's victory in the 2008 presidential election, a friend of mine forwarded an email that contained a joke that he apparently intended me to also find funny. It read: "Drink plenty of water because there's going to be a lot of salty crackers." Besides suggesting that a large number of whites resent the outcome of the election, it also encourages Obama supporters, especially black ones, to be on guard against racial and social retaliation.

The message disturbed me.

My friend is white, middle class, a husband and father of two. He was born and raised, and currently lives, in California. And for the whole long time I've known him, he's voted Republican. Now he sends an e-mail, disclosing his vote for Barack Obama and casting other whites in a negative, even intolerant, light?

I wondered: "What is this all about?"

To boot, this is the same friend who, a few years before, sent an e-mail that outlined the traits of best friends. One example presented was "the kid from kindergarten that traded his crayon with you when all that was left in the box was the ugly black one."

I was bothered by this e-mail because my friend was unwittingly participating in the racist construction of blacks. For no adjective accompanied crayons of other colors, but the word associated with the color black—ugly!—was so disparaging. In this instance, my friend was also perpetuating white privilege.

As you know, white privilege describes advantages whites commonly enjoy that are not equally extended to nonwhite people. The American standard of beauty is an example. It is based on images of white people, whereas symbols of black people often are negatively rendered. I think we'll agree that white privilege is not exactly the same as racism, since people like my friend may try to resist racist beliefs. Even so, prejudice definitely stems from white privilege.

This is why my friend's postelection e-mail was disturbing, not because he's upholding white privilege, but because he's participating in the opposite—what I'm going to call "black revenge." *Cracker* is a combined racial and class slur often used by whites and blacks to describe whites from lower income statuses who sometimes express unfiltered negative beliefs about minorities. It is also used to represent how blacks view whites from any economic class that may unfairly antagonize them. Using the term against unknown white voters and citizens puts blacks in the same cruel and antagonistic roles they resist and hope to eliminate. What makes the joke a manifestation of questionable privilege, the privilege to be counterracist, is that it was being freely circulated on the Internet without intellectual challenge or critique. At least I didn't see any challenge to it.

From my perspective, both white privilege and black revenge breed prejudice and resentment. So I felt that if my friend truly believes in "change" and "hope," the catchphrases of Obama's campaign, then he can't believe change is recycling the same hatred in a new package. He can't believe that "hope" comes from making bullies out of people who have been historically oppressed. Supporting jokes, slurs, or any language and action that's biased against white people is wrong because prejudice itself is wrong. The ongoing work is to eliminate prejudice in all forms, not simply to replace the face of the oppressed. I'm sure you agree.

This is not a kumbaya, turn-the-other-cheek perspective. For as long as whites ignore the fact of their privilege and insist on it, that insistence should be resisted. I know some who might read my friend's e-mail in a more favorable light, as a sign of willingness to give up his racial privilege. If that's true, his desire is a good thing, necessary even. I just hope he finds a more constructive way to do it.

I think what both of us, and what the antiracism movement in its best moments, are trying to do is to offer very solid ways of pursuing antiracist work that does not assign the very privilege to people of color that we take away from whites. We're not engaging in unfair maligning of whites. When we're at our best, we're deeply interrogating and analyzing whiteliness. In this context, I think of Tim Wise's important but not unproblematic work. In his book *Between Barack and a Hard Place: Racism and White Denial in the Age of Obama* (2009), he ends with several concrete steps that whites interested in pursuing antiracism should take. He writes:

> Whites must take personal responsibility for addressing racism and white privilege (116);
>
> Whites must learn to listen to (and believe) what people of color say about racism, especially in their own lives (120);
>
> Whites must be willing to hear (and grapple with) the oft-spoken but real and disturbing history of their nation when it comes to race (131);
>
> Whites should discover and connect to the unheralded but significant historical tradition of antiracist white allyship" (146–7).

I admire your project because it is doing what Wise suggests in quite specific ways, in the very context that is supposed to help level the playing field for everyone—school—and in the discipline that is the very foundation for education—reading and writing instruction. You urge whites to take personal responsibility for racism and white privilege, showing how well-meaning, even antiracist, whites must do this, must critique their whiteliness, which is not the same thing as racism, but does often have the same results. You also urge listening to what people of color have to say, and you are yourself listening, engaging in both a retrospective listening with the stories about your brother and allowing those remembrances to intensify your hearing of people of color in the present. You are also grappling with

American history in the midst of your academic and personal interrogation. And you stand, at least for me, as an example of a white ally in the tradition of antiracist work. This is a history that is important to connect to and highlight because too often whites believe this work is only for people of color. Whites may not see and are not regularly taught their personal racial histories and connections to antiracist work. So Black History Month becomes only for blacks and Latino Heritage Month becomes only for Latinos. And this kind of division is too bad and does not promote crosscultural understanding, when it has the very real potential to do so.

But, Frankie, I do have one ending concern, one that I was alarmed to see Wise succumb to in his book, but one that I think, in your case, these letters of ours address. Under the section where Wise writes that whites must take personal responsibility for white privilege, he says that "if whites will not listen to voices from black and brown communities, then fine, they will have to hear it from their own. And not just once, but over and again" (2009, 119). I really appreciate this point, because, as I've said before, and have noticed so many times, that whites don't really hear, or may stop hearing, or sometimes can't always hear what people of color have to say on issues of race. So it becomes important for whites to say it so that other whites will hear it. James Baldwin once put this strongly, when he said that black people need witnesses. But, see, Frankie, my wonder is, must black people and people of color always have a white witness to authorize our voices? Are whites the only legitimizing voice on issues of race? And will people of color continue to be afraid to speak up and out? Will they only do so if a white ally speaks? I mean, how do we get to a point where this veil on diverse voices is lifted forever?

I find Wise's advice to be troubling, even as I admire his call, because he calls for more whites to speak (a good thing), but then says, "Just maybe they will even begin to hear it from people of color, once they realize that their own sons and daughters and nephews and nieces are saying the same thing" (2009, 119).

I feel like here he is dropping the ball, leaving it too much to chance, not really carving out the space for listening to people of color. This is why I'm delighted that you invited a person of color to write with you, to share the discussion of this issue in the midst of your own work! It didn't have to be me. But I'm glad it was, glad to have this experience to wrangle, to demonstrate, not by simulation but by actual engagement and practice, how we can work together toward an *anti*racist society and stick with it, even when it is sticky, quite risky.

Thank you for the experience, friend, and Godspeed to you and to your—oops! I mean "to our"—work!

AFTERWORD

Years ago, Elizabeth Boquet was the keynote speaker at a National Conference on Peer Tutoring in Writing held in Lawrence, Kansas. The conference organizers had arranged a band for the conference reception. During one of their sets, Beth stepped up to the microphone, and to the band's accompaniment sang an extraordinarily beautiful rendition of Curtis Mayfield's song, "People Get Ready."

People get ready, there's a train a comin'
You don't need no baggage, you just get on board
All you need is faith to hear the diesels hummin'
Don't need no ticket, you just thank the Lord

People get ready for the train to Jordan
It's picking up passengers from coast to coast
Faith is the key, open the doors and board 'em
There's hope for all among those loved the most.

There ain't no room for the hopeless sinner
Who would hurt all mankind just to save his own
Have pity on those whose chances grow thinner
For there's no hiding place against the Kingdom's throne

So people get ready, there's a train a comin'
You don't need no baggage, you just get on board
All you need is faith to hear the diesels hummin'
Don't need no ticket, you just thank the Lord

(Curtis Mayfield 1965)[1]

1. "People Get Ready" lyrics. Curtis Mayfield. *LyricsMania*, http://www.lyrics-mania.com/people_get_ready_lyrics_curtis_mayfield.html.

I have always loved this song. I love the slow gospel roll of Mayfield's version sung with the Impressions. I love the heartachingly beautiful sound of Eva Cassidy's version. And when Beth sang, I heard the song in yet another and new way. It was Beth who, in *Noise from the Writing Center*, sent me to the question of what it means to get ready as a writer, as a teacher, as a tutor. As she sang the song that night, I thought about Curtis Mayfield, about the world into and for which the song was written. I thought about Beth's work and her attentiveness to "the *ready* of ready, set, go" (Geller et al., 2007, 22; italics in original). I thought about the antiracist leadership training in which I was immersed at the time. And Beth's version of the song, offered so unexpectedly on that night, as I worried over my ability to articulate what I was learning about antiracism during my upcoming conference presentation, helped me connect my sense of what it means to get ready to my sense of the work that composes the epistemologies and rhetorics antiracist activism.

I write these words and am tempted to explain away, to excuse, the fact that it took a white woman singing for me to hear—really hear—the ways in which Mayfield's song speaks to the work to which I have attached so much importance as a woman, as a mother and daughter and sister, as a scholar, teacher, writer, and activist. I'll point to the context, I think to myself, as I remember the night she sang. I *happened* to be thinking of all these things on that night and so it's an accident. And so it may be at some level. But as Vershawn points out in the last letter we've shared with you, such accidents seem to occur with alarming regularity for those of us most closely attended by whiteliness as we think, speak, and write. Just to be clear: it wasn't Beth singing the song that caused the problem. It was me; it was my openness to hearing in her voice the import of Mayfield's words and that which I had been unwilling or unable to hear from a man of color, even someone I had professed to be a hero of mine, that caused that "accident."

Here is deep matter, and Vay is not alone in calling us to attend to it: those of us who are white and are committed to the work of antiracism must know that we bear a tremendous responsibility to bear witness, to testify, and to join with peoples of color in the struggle for racial equality. But we must also know that to do such work does not free us from our own implicatedness either in the enactment or the reproduction of racism. Further, neither our witness nor our testimony should ever supplant in our own minds or in our articulations, by implication or design, the stories and the testimonies of peoples of color.

And yet, they will. Some whites will be moved by what we speak and write, and how we speak and write, in ways they have refused to be moved by peoples of color speaking and writing of the same matters in similar ways. And, if we are honest, I suspect we will recognize that we are guilty of the same sin. This reality does not mean we ought not speak out nor write. Silence is not a viable alternative. The practices of decentering, nuancing, and storying the raced dimensions of our lives in the deep time of a big here and a long now might enable us to recognize, name, and transgress the rules of racial standing that lead us to whitely habits of believing and doubting. As we choose to whom we will listen, we are choosing our people—choosing those with whom we will affiliate, with whom we will join as we move through the world collectively creating the legacies we will leave for our descendants. To learn and relearn in endless iterations endlessly the epistemologies and rhetorics of antiracism is to learn to choose differently. Maybe in the embrace of uncertainties engendered by these practices we really can, as Powell writes, "learn to take hold of one another and emerge at the beginning of a new story about ourselves, not a 'prime' narrative held together by the sameness of our beliefs, but a gathering of narratives," together at the joint (2004, 58).

My daughter, Lucy, my middle child (Lucy, who is different than me and has begun to notice the differences), has taken to asking me lately, many times a day, "Mama, do you love me?" "Mama, do you love *me*?" "Mama, do *you* love me?" I try to answer. "Lucy," I say, "I *love* you! I love *you*! *I* love you!" I think about how to answer her better all the time. In my imagination,

I try to elaborate, to catch hold of the ineffable, the unutterable, and to speak it. "Lucy," I imagine saying (and maybe I will say someday), "The world tells me that I'm supposed to love you because I'm a woman. The world tells me I'm supposed to love you because I'm your mother. The world tells me I'm supposed to love you because you were conceived in me. The world tells me I'm supposed to love you because my blood fed you until you could feed yourself, because while you were in me our blood mingled together, was one blood." I imagine saying what I wish my family, my community, I, could have said to my brother. I imagine saying to Lucy, "Fuck blood. Blood splits us, divides us; blood is not and never has been love. Let us re-member ourselves along love's lines. I choose you. You choose me too. I dance wildly when you are with me. I laugh until I cry. I sing and don't care how I sound so long as you are smiling. I will love you forever and for always and not because anyone tells me I should. And blood will have nothing to do with our love. Blood won't be the condition by which I'll love you because there will be no, there are no, conditions. I choose you. *I* do LOVE *you.*

There is, I believe, no racial identity (no any kind of identity) so determined, so essential that we cannot make the choice to love and, in that loving, lose our sense of oneness, of singularity, of positioning at the self-end of the self/other binary. This loss, which is also racism's loss, constitutes a yield that both opposes and transcends self-interest; it is a harvest bountiful enough to feed all our relations.

The greatest risk of antiracism work, so far as I can tell, is the risk of never beginning, of not doing it at all. And that's a danger that emanates not from some imaginary villain over there in the administration building; or upstairs in the office of the chair; or across the hall in the faculty lounge; or in the big white halls of power in Washington DC; or down the streets of our neighborhoods; nor even from the white-sheeted figure haunting our memory and our imagination. The danger, the risk of never beginning, is programmed into *us* as the idea that there is nothing to be gained that might outweigh the risks, that our own *skins* are more valuable than anybody else's and that we ought to save our *skins* no matter what the cost. That risk comes from us, it's in us. The only way I know to face that risk and to account for it is to turn to remember the past; to recognize the traces of the past in the present and in you; to acknowledge your own pain and the pain of others without accounting yours the more pressing or distressing; to admit the partiality of your ability to know yourself and others; to prepare for the making of mistakes; to practice compassion for yourself and others; and to speak the truth as best you can discern it and to speak that truth to power. And while you're doing all of that, you do the work: partially, incompletely, inadequately, but always with the certainty that others will come after you to whom you owe your care in thinking, speaking, writing, and doing such that they can carry on toward the invention of the greatest unknown of all: justice. That's all. And it really is as simple and as terrible as that. This is a love letter to a world in which love is not enough, but only the beginning: the tender, tremulous reach toward the possibility that we might all one day join the band.

REFERENCES

Ahmed, Sara. 2004. Declarations of whiteness: The non-performativity of anti-racism, *Borderlands* 3.2: http://www.borderlands.net.au/vol3no2_2004/ahmed_declarations.htm.

Aptheker, Herbert. 1993. *Anti-Racism in U.S. History: The First 200 Years.* Praeger Paperback.

Alcoff, Linda. 2007. Epistemologies of ignorance: Three types. In *Race and epistemologies of ignorance,* edited by Shannon Sullivan and Nancy Tuana. Albany: State University of New York Press.

———. 2005. *Visible identities: Race, gender, and the self.* Oxford: Oxford University Press.

Anzaldúa, Gloria. 1999. *Borderlands/la frontera: The new mestiza.* San Francisco: Aunt Lute Books.

Baldwin, James. 1985. *The price of the ticket: Collected nonfiction 1948-1985.* New York: St. Martins/Marek.

Barr, Robert B., and John Tagg. 2003. A new paradigm for undergraduate education. *Change Magazine,* November/December, page.

Barthes, Roland. 1980. *Camera lucida: Reflections on photography.* New York: Hill & Wang.

———. 1979. *A lover's discourse: Fragments.* New York: Hill & Wang.

Bell, Derrick. 1992. *Faces at the bottom of the well: The permanence of racism.* New York: Basic Books. 1989. *And we are not saved: The elusive quest for racial justice.* New York: Basic Books.

Bonilla-Silva, Eduardo. 2006. *Racism without racists: Color-blind racism and the persistence of racial inequality in the United States.* 2nd ed. Rowman & Littlefield.

Booth, James W. 2006. *Communities of memory: On witness, identity, and justice.* Ithaca, NY: Cornell University Press.

Boquet, Elizabeth. 2001. *Noise from the writing center.* Logan: Utah State University Press.

Branch, Kirk. 2007. *Eyes on the ought to be: What we teach when we teach about literacy.* New York: Hampton Press.

Butler, Judith. 2005. *Giving an account of oneself.* New York: Fordham University Press.

Carse, James. 1987. *Finite and infinite games: A vision of life as play and possibility.* New York: Random House. 2009. *The religious case against belief.* New York: The Penguin Press. Kindle edition.

Churchill, Ward. 2004. *Kill the Indian, save the man: The genocidal impact of American Indian residential schools.* San Francisco: City Lights Publishers.

Condon, Frankie. 2007. Beyond the known: Writing centers and the work of anti-racism. *Writing Center Journal* 27.2: 19-38.

Corder, James. 1985. Argument as emergence, rhetoric as love. *Rhetorical Review* 4, no. 1: 16–32.

Crosswhite, James. 1996. *The rhetoric of reason: Writing and the attractions of argument.* Madison: University of Wisconsin Press.

Deming, Barbara. On anger. accessed October 18, 2011. http://homepage.mac.com/deyestone/onanger.html.

Digh, Patricia. 2005. We need to stop creating tame solutions for wicked problems—like racism. *The Circle Project.* http://37days.typepad.com/thecircleproject/avoidance/.

Eno, Brian. 2001. The big here and the long now. *digital souls.com.* http://www.digitalsouls.com/2001/Brian_Eno_Big_Here.html. .

Ethnic studies ban racist? 2011. *CNN Homepage.* http://www.cnn.com/video/data/2.0/video/bestoftv/2010/05/12/ac.ethics.study.ban.cnn.html.

Fox, Catherine. 2002. The race to truth: Disarticulating critical thinking from whiteliness. *Pedagogy* 2, no. 2: 197–212.

Frazer, James George. 1935. *The golden bough.* New York: Macmillan.

Frye, Marilyn. 2001. White woman feminist 1983–1992. In *Race and racism,* edited by Bernard Boxill. Oxford: Oxford University Press.

Gee, James Paul. 2001. Literacy, discourse, and linguistics. In *Literacy: A critical sourcebook,* edited by Ellen Cushman, Eugene R. Kintgen, Barry M. Kroll, and Mike Rose. New York: Bedford/St. Martin's.

Geller, Anne Ellen, Michele Eodice, Frankie Condon, Meg Carroll, and Elizabeth Boquet. 2007. *The everyday writing center: A community of practice.* Logan: Utah State University Press.

Gilyard, Keith ed. 1999. *Race, rhetoric, and composition.* Portsmouth: Boynton/Cook.

Graff, Gerald. 2011. "Code-meshing meets teaching the conflicts," in *Code-meshing as world English: pedagogy, policy, performance,* edited by Vershawn Ashanti Young and Aja Y. Martinez. NCTE: 9-20.

Grimberg, Sharon, et al. 2009. We shall remain: America through Native eyes. Episode 5: Wounded Knee. DVD. Boston : WGBH Educational Foundation.

Grimm, Nancy. 1999. Good intentions: Writing center work for postmodern times. Portsmouth: Boynton/Cook.

Grudin, Robert. 1997. Time and the art of living. Boston and New York: Mariner Books.

Herman, Ellen. 2007. Indian adoption project. *The Adoption History Project.* http://darkwing.uoregon.edu/~adoption/topics/IAP.html.

Holt Marilyn Irvin. 2004. *Indian orphanages.* Lawrence: University of Kansas Press.

Horton, Myles. 1990. We make the road by walking: Conversations on education and social change. Philadelphia: Temple University Press.

Huey, Aaron. http://www.tumblr.com/tagged/Lakota; accessed Nov. 14, 2010.

Kahane, Adam. 2010. *Power and love: A theory and practice of social change.* Place of publication: Berrett-Koehler. Kindle edition.

King, Martin Luther. 1967. The Southern Christian Leadership Conference presidential address. *World History Archives.* http://www.hartford-hwp.com/archives/45a/628.html.

King, Elizabeth. 1999. *Attention's loop: A sculptor's reverie on the coexistence of substance and spirit.* New York: Harry N. Abrams, Inc.

Leopold, Aldo. Thinking like a mountain. *Dead Trees EF!* Accessed March 19, 2011. http://www.eco-action.org/dt/thinking.html.

Lyons, Scott Richard. 2000. Rhetorical sovereignty: What do American Indians want from writing. *College Composition and Communication* 51, no. 3: 447–468.

Lu, Min-Zhan. 1999. Redefining the literate self: The politics of critical affirmation. *College Composition and Communication* 51, no. 2: 172–194.

Maclear, Kyo. 1998. *Beclouded visions: Hiroshima-Nagasaki and the art of witness.* Albany: State University of New York Press.

Margalit, Avishai. 2002. *The ethics of memory.* Cambridge: Harvard University Press.

Matthiessen, Peter. 1992. *In the spirit of Crazy Horse.* New York: Penguin Books.

Messr-Davidow, Ellen. 2002. *Disciplining feminism: From social activism to academic discourse.* Durham, NC: Duke University Press.

Mills, Charles. 1999. *The Racial Contract.* Ithica, NY: Cornell University Press.

O'Connor, Flannery. 1992. Revelation. In *The complete stories.* New York: Noonday Press, Farrar, Straus and Giroux.

Omi, Michael, and Howard Winant. 1994. *Racial formation in the United States: From the 1960s to the 1990s.* London: Routledge.

Parks, Sharon Daloz. 2000. *Big questions worthy dreams: mentoring young adults in their search for meaning, purpose, and faith.* San Francisco: Jossey-Bass.

Passover. *aish.com.* http://www.aish.com/h/pes/h/48954191.html. Accessed April 2, 2011. http://www.aish.com/h/pes/h/48954191.html.

Powell, Malea. 2004. Down by the river, or how Susan La Flesche Picotte can teach us about alliance as a practice of survivance. Special issue, *College English* 67, no. 1: 38–60.

———. 2002. Rhetorics of survivance: How American Indians use writing. *College Composition and Communication* 53, no. 3: 396–434.

Pratt, Minnie Bruce, Elly Bulkin, and Barbara Smith. 1988. *Yours in struggle: Three feminist perspectives on anti-semitism and racism.* Ithaca, NY: Firebrand Books.

Probyn, Elspeth. 2005. *Blush: Faces of shame.* Minneapolis: University of Minnesota Press.

Ratcliffe, Krista. 2006. *Rhetorical listening: Identification, gender, whiteness.* Carbondale: Southern Illinois University Press.

Richardson, Elaine. 2003. *African American literacies.* London: Routledge.

———. 2002. To Protect and Serve: African American female literacies. *College Composition and Communication* 53, no. 4: 675–704.

Sandoval, Chela. 2000. Methodology of the oppressed. Vol. 18 of *Theory out of bounds.* Minneapolis: University of Minnesota Press.

Solnit, Rebecca. 2005. *A field guide to getting lost.* London: Viking.

Stuckey, J. Elspeth. 1990. *The violence of literacy.* Portsmouth, NH: Boynton/Cook.

Tillich, Paul. 1960. *Love, power, and justice: Ontological analyses and ethical applications.* Oxford: Oxford University Press.

Treaty of Fort Laramie with Sioux etc. 1851. Indian affairs: Laws and treaties. Digital Libraries of Oklahoma State University. Accessed September 17, 2010. http://digital.library.okstate.edu/kappler/vol2/treaties/sio0594.htm.

Treaty with the Sioux: Brule, Oglala, Miniconjou, Yanktonai, Hunkpapa, Blackfeet, Cuthead, Two Kettle, Sans Arcs, Santee—and Arapahoe. 1868. Digital Libraries of Oklahoma State University. Accessed April 29, 2010.

http://digital.library.okstate.edu/kappler/vol2/treaties/sio0998.htm.

Tri-Council Coordinating Commission and the Minnesota Collaborative Anti-Racism Initiative. 2004. *Minneapolis MN Crossroads and TCC/MCARI. Anti-Racism Team Organizer's Manual.* Unpublished.

Villanueva, Victor. 2006. Blind: Racism and responsibility. *Writing Center Journal* 26.1: 3–19.

———. 2004. Memoria is a friend of ours: On the discourse of color. *College English* 67, no. 1: 9–19.

Vizenor, Gerald. 1994. *Manifest manners: Narratives on post-Indian survivance.* Lincoln: University of Nebraska Press.

———. 2009. *Native liberty: Natural reason and cultural survivance.* Lincoln: University of Nebraska Press. Kindle edition.

———. 1993. Trickster discourse: Tragic and comic themes in Native American literature. In *Buried roots and indestructible seeds: The survival of American Indian life in story, history, and spirit.* Edited by Mark A. Lindquist and Martin Zanger. Madison: University of Wisconsin Press.

West, Cornel. 2005. Prisoner of hope. *CommonDreams.org.* http://www.commondreams.org/views05/0111-35.htm.

Wetherell, Margaret and Jonathan Potter. 1993. *Mapping the language of racism: Discourse and the legitimation of exploitation.* New York: Columbia University Press.

Williams, Patricia. 1992. *Alchemy of race and rights: Diary of a law professor.* Cambridge: Harvard University Press.

Wise, Tim. 2009. *Between Barack and a hard place.* San Francisco: City Lights Publishers.

Young, Vershawn Ashanti. 2010. Momma's memories and the new equality. *Present Tense* 1, no. 1. http://www.presenttensejournal.org/vol1/momma%E2%80%99s-memories-and-the-new-equality/

———. 2007. *Your average nigga: Performing race, literacy, and masculinity.* Detroit: Wayne State University Press.

Young, Vershawn Ashanti, and Aja Y. Martinez, eds. *Code-meshing as world English: Pedagogy, policy, performance.* Urbana, IL: NCTE, forthcoming.

INDEX

ABOUT THE AUTHORS

FRANKIE CONDON is an associate professor of English and the faculty coordinator of the writing center at the University of Nebraska-Lincoln. She lives in Lincoln with her husband, Mike, her three children, Dan, Lucy, and Grace, her mom, Suzy, and two dogs, a cat, and two chinchillas. Her published work includes *The Everyday Writing Center: A Community of Practice*, coauthored with Michele Eodice, Elizabeth Boquet, Anne Ellen Geller, and Meg Carroll. Frankie's essays have appeared in the *Writing Center Journal, Praxis, College Teaching*, and *Junctures*.

VERSHAWN A. YOUNG is an associate professor of African American studies and English at the University of Kentucky—is an interdisciplinary artist-critic. He writes about African American language, literature, gender, race, and performance, and often stages his research as one-man shows. His publications include *Your Average Nigga: Performing Race, Literacy, and Masculinity* (2007); *From Bourgeois to Boojie: Black Middle-Class Performances* (2011); and *Code-Meshing as World English: Pedagogy, Policy, Performance* with Aja Y. Martinez (2011). He is currently at work on *Straight Black Queers: Gender Anxiety and the American Dream*, a book that examines the masculine and feminine angst exhibited by successful African Americans such as Barack Obama, Michelle Obama, playwright August Wilson, and journalist Leanita McClain.